# THE LOST JOURNAL OF
# BRAM STOKER

⊷ THE DUBLIN YEARS ⊶

# THE LOST JOURNAL OF
# BRAM STOKER

EDITED BY

⊷ ELIZABETH MILLER ⊶
& DACRE STOKER

**The Robson Press**

Published in Great Britain in 2012 by
The Robson Press
Biteback Publishing Ltd
Westminster Tower
3 Albert Embankment
London SE1 7SP

ISBN 978-1-84954-188-6

10 9 8 7 6 5 4 3 2 1

A CIP catalogue record for this book is available from the
British Library.

Set in Caslon and Filosofia by Namkwan Cho
Cover design by Namkwan Cho

Printed and bound in Great Britain by
CPI Group (UK) Ltd, Croydon CR0 4YY

*To Bram, Florence and Noel Stoker*

# A Damned Lie

I once knew a little boy who put so many flies in a bottle that they had not room to die!!!

2/10/72

A clever man once copper bottomed the top of his house with sheet-lead.

26/1/73

Dean _____ of Manchester once in marrying 200 couples on Easter Monday made some mistake & join the wrong people throughout the whole series. When remonstrated with by some of the parties he said = "Well never mind now. You can sort each other when you get outside.

26/4/73

# ⇒ CONTENTS ⇐

# ⊷ PHOTOS & ⊶
# ILLUSTRATIONS

Cover photo – Bram Stoker Estate

Photo of Elizabeth Miller & Dacre Stoker at
Greystones (inside flap) – photo by Brian J. Showers

**Plate Section**

*Noel Dobbs*
Bram Stoker's Journal

*Dublin City Library and Archive*
Theatre Royal

*John Moore Collection*
Abraham Stoker; Charlotte Stoker; Richard Stoker;

copy of *Under the Sunset*; copy of *The Snake's Pass*; copy of *A Glimpse of America*; copy of *Dracula*, 1912; skeleton sketch of Bram Stoker; page from *The Duties of Clerks of Petty Sessions in Ireland*; sketch of Bram Stoker fishing; mini-photos of Bram Stoker for Chapters 1, 2 (from *Penny Illustrated* magazine), 3, 6 (from *Literary Lounger*), 7, 8 and 9.

*Illustrated London News* (20 June 1874)
A foot race in College Park, Dublin

*National Gallery of Ireland*
Painting ('Dublin Castle Gate') by Samuel Brocas; painting ('Going to the Levee') by Rose Barton; painting ('The New Post Office and the Pillar, Sackville Street') by Thomas Sautell Roberts, Havell & Son.

Ceri Oakes, *Whitby Gazette*
Mini-photo of Bram Stoker, Chapter 4.

*Rosenbach Museum & Library*
Page from Bram Stoker's Notes for *Dracula*.

*The Royal Fleet Auxiliary Historical Society*
Royal Humane Society Bronze Medal

*The Board of Trinity College Dublin* (TCD MUN SOC HIST 86)
Bram with other officers of the Historical Society

All other images are the property of the Bram Stoker Estate, with contributions from Patrick McG. Stoker.

**Integrated Images**

p. 104:
'Dublin Castle' by Richard Dowling (1871).

p. 122:
'A Treatise on Fever, with Observations on the Practice Adopted for its Cure, in the Fever Hospital and House of Recovery in Dublin' by William Stoker, MD (1815).

p. 163:
'Dreadful Fire with Loss of Life in Dublin' from *The Annual Register, A Review of Public Events at Home and Abroad* (1866).

p. 255:
'Mabille's Faded Glory', *New York Times* (September 1, 1878).

p. 272:
'The Forest of Dean' by Arthur Owens Cooke (1913).

Abraham Stoker

1. August 1871

# ⇥ INTRODUCTION ⇤

The year 2012 marks the centenary of Bram Stoker's death. Interest in Stoker still tends to focus on him as the author of *Dracula*, his 1897 masterpiece. But in recent decades scholars have gone beyond his Gothic novel to assess the significance of his other works, especially his novels and short stories. Relevant to this book are efforts to present Stoker as an Irish writer. Many naysayers, however, still contend that even though Stoker wrote one novel set in Ireland (*The Snake's Pass*), he completely ignored Dublin, the city where he spent the first thirty years of his life. He still has never quite 'made it' as a literary Dubliner.

Now all of that is about to change. This Journal contains 310 individual entries of varying lengths written on about 160 pages over an eleven-year period (1871–1882). At least 285 of the entries were recorded before he left Dublin for London at the end of 1878. Indeed, Dublin stands centre-stage as Stoker provides details about his life in the city: his colleagues at Dublin Castle, his classmates at Trinity College, his early attraction to the theatre (long before he met Henry Irving), his observations of the Dublin street, and above all, his rich, Irish sense of humour. There are dozens of references to friends and family; travel and office life; drunken parties, court cases and christenings. Not one of its pages has ever been published until now.

Above all, this Journal is a commonplace book, a writer's companion, a grab bag for a variety of descriptions, anecdotes, quotations, observations and musings. Sometimes Bram writes in the first person, while at other times he comments as a detached observer, or transmits someone else's accounts. Especially noteworthy are the jottings of an emerging writer as he keeps a record of themes, plots and characters for future use in his fiction. There are even foreshadowings of *Dracula*. Many of the entries provide tantalising insights into the man himself – his social life, his character, his sensitivity, his moral values, his Gothic sensibility and above all his Irishness.

## PROVENANCE

At present the Journal resides on a bookshelf on the Isle of Wight, in the home of Noel Dobbs, Bram Stoker's great-grandson. Noel provides this account of its journey:

> The Journal was among the books left to me by my grandfather Noel [Stoker]. My grandfather's books included what must have been some of the contents of Bram's library, which was presumably left to my great-grandmother, Florence Stoker, after Bram's death in 1912. The route for this Journal was therefore as follows: Florence – Noel – me.

But for decades it languished in obscurity, its existence unknown to the world of Stoker/*Dracula* scholars and fans alike, until it was discovered by Noel Dobbs about ten years ago. Other than providing access to Paul Murray, who incorporated elements of it into his biography *From the Shadow of Dracula: A Life of Bram Stoker* (London: Jonathan Cape, 2004), the Journal has remained inaccessible. Only now are its full contents being made publicly available, thanks to Noel Dobbs's decision to grant us the rights to its publication.

## DESCRIPTION

Dark reddish brown in colour, the hardcover Journal comprises pages about 8x6 inches in size. There is no text on the cover. On the inside front cover Bram has pasted

*Abraham Stoker*
1 August 1871

Entries are written on recto side only, starting with 2 and running for 164 pages (four of which are absent or blank). There are over thirty blank pages at the back. Ninety of the entries are dated, the earliest 3.8.71 (3 August 1871), the latest 4.6.82 (4 June 1882). The majority of dated entries are from the period 1871–1873. There is no pattern discernible in the frequency of entries: at times, two or three are made in the same day, while elsewhere there are gaps of weeks or months between entries. They are, for the most part, chronological – but not always. Occasionally, Bram transcribed items from an earlier dated note. Eight loose pages have been inserted at the back. The fact that they are of different size and/or colour of paper shows that they are not physically part of the Journal.

In *Personal Reminiscences of Henry Irving* (1906), Bram mentions a 'pocket-book': 'Lest I should forget the exact words I wrote them then and there in my pocket-book. I entered them later in my diary' (vol. 2, p. 2). Apparently, he carried such an item around with him – with, one presumes, a pencil – and made preliminary entries 'on the spot', followed up later by Journal entries in pen. This pattern of writing is further indicated by the times of day he records on a few of the entries.

## METHODOLOGY

In preparing the Journal for publication, we were confronted with two major challenges. The first was to decipher Bram's handwriting. As he once admitted, 'I write in an extremely bad hand' (*Personal Reminiscences*, vol. 1, p. 42). For the most part, however, with effort and patience, we have been able to transcribe most of the handwritten text. About a dozen words and phrases still baffle us. We have drawn attention to these by using the designation <xxx>. For the purposes of clarity, we have performed some light editing of the original text (mostly punctuation), though no changes of substance have been made.

Our second task was to determine how to arrange and present the material. We first considered transcribing the Journal in the sequence in which Stoker wrote the entries. But we soon realised that doing so would make the task of commenting and interpreting virtually impossible, given the disparate nature of the subject matter from one entry to the next. We therefore opted for grouping the entries by subject/theme. Each chapter comprises not only the relevant transcriptions but also our commentary/analysis and extensive annotations. These are augmented by facsimiles of several pages of the original Journal. We also provide illustrative material (much of which has not been published before), including – at the beginning of each chapter – nine photos of Bram Stoker spanning fifty-five years of his life.

We have assigned consecutive numbering to each of the 310 entries. For citations from and cross-references to the entries throughout our text, we use the number (1, 2 etc.) without the designation [p.] As these are not Stoker's numbers, we are providing a key (see pp. 307–10) that matches each entry to the corresponding page number in the original Journal.

Bram's Journal is peppered with marginal notes: some are clearly in his own hand while others were entered at later dates by his wife, Florence. We are including explanations, as required, in the annotations.

We are convinced that the contents of this Journal will prove useful to future scholars researching and writing about Bram Stoker. We hope to open doors so that others can pick up the trail and solve any outstanding mysteries.

# ➡ACKNOWLEDGEMENTS⬅

Dacre Stoker and I wish to acknowledge the significant contributions of several individuals who helped during this project. First we thank Noel Dobbs, Bram Stoker's great-grandson, who not only provided facsimile images of the entire Journal but also gave us exclusive publishing rights. As the project proceeded, his assistance in answering our many questions proved invaluable.

We also appreciate the support and assistance of other members of the Stoker family, notably Robin MacCaw and Patrick McG. Stoker. Deserving of special mention is Douglas S. Appleyard, Dublin-based historian and Stoker genealogist, who is related to the Stokers through a cousin of Bram's father.

Jenne Stoker put her exceptional research skills to

8

good use, providing us with copious notes on people, places and events mentioned in the annotations and the timeline. Her keen eye helped us decipher some of the more illegible of Bram's notes.

And then there is our 'Blessed Trinity': John Moore, Carol A. Senf and Brian J. Showers. From the outset, the three of them agreed to come on board as researchers and readers. The wealth of information and advice provided by this trio was immense. Specifically, John, a collector, gave us access to his remarkable archive of Stoker material; Carol, an English professor at the Georgia Institute of Technology, filled in our gaps about Stoker's works other than *Dracula*; and Brian, 'our man in Dublin', not only supplied us with invaluable information about Dublin but also traipsed along with us as we visited every conceivable Stoker site in that fair city.

*Elizabeth Miller*
January 2012

## Night fishing

A grey sky. broken by dark patches of cloud. that make
even the grey look bright – A low line of of light along the
horizon on the East . A dark grey sea luminous towards the
horizon – just before Moonrise . A line of surf along the
shore . A low west wind sighing softly by the sea side.
The fishermen dragging their nets . in silence . The nets as they
from the water are starred with phosphorescent lights. as the
ends of the net come nearer & the lead line comes up upon
the beach the fish are seen struggling in the net & show
their white bellies through the shallow water. The fishermen pass
round the back of the net and lift & push it inshore in
every wave – Across the sea gleam the light houses some
fixed some rising to life blazing full. and then becoming again
invisible. Bray head looks black against the sky. A few winking
gleams still on shore – From the chinks of a fisherman's door
come dull rays of light and there is no sound save the
ceaseless wash of the waves & the gentle sighing of the wind. These
we heed not as sounds – but we do hear the occasional rumble
a vehicle along some road inshore – Unconsciously and &
instinctively we remain silent

Greystones . 3.8.71 1. A.M.

# ONE

# ⟜ASPIRING WRITER⟞

August 1, 1871 was a red-letter day for Bram Stoker. That was the date he inscribed on a notebook into which he would make hundreds of entries over the following ten years. It is the starting point for tracing his journey as a writer. At the age of twenty-three, he was living at the time in the family home at 43 Harcourt St., Dublin. He had graduated from Trinity College in the previous year with a BA and would acquire the Master's degree five years later. An active student in both athletics and intellectual pursuits, he maintained his connections with the College for several years after graduation. Most significant was his continued participation in the activities of both the Philosophical and Historical societies. For example, only the year before (in 1870) he had delivered a lecture entitled 'Means of Improvement in Composition'. In addition, earlier in 1871 he had vigorously defended the poetry of Walt Whitman at a meeting of the 'Phil'. He kept close contact with many of his university friends, several of whom make brief appearances throughout the Journal.

In August 1871, having followed dutifully in the path towards respectability laid out for him by his father, he was employed as a civil servant at the Department of Registrar of Petty Sessions Clerks, Dublin Castle. He was still using the name 'Abraham' which he shared with his father. He would not adopt the more informal 'Bram' until after his father's death in 1876, an outward sign of his breaking free, shedding the weight of both name and expectations.

In his position at Dublin Castle, Bram spent many hours tediously recording and filing reports from the petty sessions courts. His income was necessary to supplement his father's pension at a time when three of his brothers were being educated in medicine. His Journal allowed him to express his creative side without offending his father. In 1871 he was on the threshold of what would be a long and successful stint as a writer and a theatre man.

Later that year he began writing regular theatre reviews for the *Dublin Evening Mail*, an activity that would lead in time to a lengthy and successful business relationship with the British actor, Henry Irving. In 1872, his first short story was published. 'The Crystal Cup', which appeared in the periodical *London Society*, tells of an imprisoned artist – maybe a metaphor for himself at Dublin Castle. Three years later it was followed by several episodes of stories in *The Shamrock*, a Dublin magazine, collectively entitled *The Primrose Path*. In these stories, Stoker tackles a more intense theme – alcoholism and domestic violence, both of which were all too prevalent in the Dublin of his time.

The opening entry in the Journal, entitled 'Night Fishing' (1), is the earliest example of Stoker's creative prose that we have. Essentially a word painting, it shows an aspiring writer composing an excessively descriptive passage in flowery language. We sense his personal connection with the sea and his respect for the people (including fishermen and others) who are at its mercy. He had a lifelong passion for the sea, as seen in his frequent visits later to Whitby and Cruden Bay, and his enjoyment of swimming and boating. This interest would manifest itself in some of his published works, most notably *The Watter's Mou'* (1894), *Dracula* (1897), *The Mystery of the Sea* (1902) and 'Greater Love' (1914).

'Night Fishing' was written in Greystones, a coastal town in Co. Wicklow, about twenty miles south of

Dublin. Greystones was popular in Stoker's time (and still is today) as a destination for holiday-makers. Its features include a long stretch of beach of which part is 'shingle' (i.e. stony). Evidence in other entries around the same time indicates that he and a few friends were spending an extended weekend in the coastal town. No doubt he enjoyed the opportunity to relax, away from the stress (and boredom) of daily work at Dublin Castle, and to allow his creative side to come to the surface.

Years later, Stoker would draw from his Journal for two of his early books: *Under the Sunset* (a collection of short stories for children, 1881) and *The Snake's Pass* (a novel, 1890). At one point he scribbles a memo for a story: 'A man builds up a shadow on a wall bit by bit by adding to substance. Suddenly the shadow becomes alive' (31). A marginal note confirms its later use as the kernel of a story in *Under the Sunset* entitled 'The Shadow Builder'. Another note reads: 'Palace of Fairy Queen. Child goes to sleep & palace grows – sky changes into blue silk curtains etc.' (35). Dreaming children make appearances in a number of stories in the collection, notably 'How 7 Went Mad', 'Lies and Lilies' and 'The Wondrous Child'.

Many more notes and jottings would find their way into *The Snake's Pass*, his only novel set entirely in Ireland. The book shows the influence of his frequent travels around Ireland during his tenure at Petty Sessions. Much of this material appears verbatim in the book, mostly to flesh out the comic character, Andy Sullivan. At one point Stoker even constructs a bare-bones plot for the novel (43).

We also find many suggestions for stories we assume were never written: titles such as 'The Modesty of Ignorance' (11) and 'The Musical Liar' (40), a story about a man married by proxy (45) and a tale of a letter being sent in the wrong envelope (50). Even more intriguing are the notes of a 'web-legged girl with legs like flippers of a seal' (6) and of sleeping 'under a rug of cat skins' (46). At one point he planned to write a series of narratives based on modernised myths of Venus, Mars and Vulcan (21). He hoped to dabble in allegory, farce and comedy, and he planned a second collection of children's stories (39).

Bram Stoker also tried his hand at poetry. His earliest surviving poem entitled 'Acrostic' (53) is dated 1870. There is no evidence that it was ever submitted for publication. An acrostic is a poem in which the first letter, syllable or word of each line spells out a word, name or message. In this case, the first letters spell 'Bessie L'Estrange'. (We shall return to the mysterious Bessie in Chapter 4.)

Bram's interest in poetry bore fruit in 1885, when 'One Thing Needful' became his first published poem.

Initially entitled 'Mary (3)', it appears in its original form in his Journal (38). Based on the Mary/Martha story as recorded in Luke 10:38–42, it is one of four that Stoker wrote entitled 'Mary': 'Mary (1)' tells of the death of Lazarus and how Jesus raised him from the dead (John 11:1–12:11); 'Mary (2)' is the story of Mary Magdalene and the resurrection of Jesus (based on John 20:11–17); and 'Mary (4)' returns to the Lazarus theme. Stoker may have considered these four poems as a unit. Written in similar, unfamiliar rhyme pattern – 'Spanish sestet' (aabccb) – all show signs of editing, as if they were works in progress.

Much of his poetry is imitative: for example, 'Dreamland' (3) is written in trochaic octameter, in variations of the metre used by Edgar Allan Poe in 'The Raven' and Alfred, Lord Tennyson in 'Locksley Hall'. Here we see Stoker, as many budding poets do, imitating the masters, probing common themes of sentimental poetry such as love, longing and loneliness, and expressing them with tried and true diction. The results are predictably artificial. At other times, however, he lets his imagination run free, exploring various poetic elements from simile (9) to synaesthesia (5). But we must keep in mind that Stoker was, after all, testing his skill in a private notebook, unaware that the results would be analysed 140 years later!

## TRANSCRIPTIONS

*Greystones, where Bram made his first Journal entry*

### 1

### *'Night Fishing'*

*A grey sky, broken by dark patches of cloud that make even the grey look bright. A low line of light along the horizon in the East. A dark grey sea luminous towards the horizon just before moonrise. A line of surf along the shore. A nor-west wind sighing softly by the seaside. The fishermen dragging their nets in silence. The nets as they rise from the water are starred with phosphorescent lights. As the ends of the net come nearer & the lead line comes up upon the beach, the fishes are seen struggling in the net & show their white bellies through the shallow water. The fishermen gather around the back of the net and lift & push it inshore with every wave. Across the sea gleam the lighthouses, some fixed some rising to life, blazing full and then becoming again invisible. Bay head looks black against the sky. A few windows gleam still on shore, from the chinks of a fisherman's door come dull rays of light and there is no sound save the ceaseless wash of the waves and the gentle sighing of the wind. These we heed not as sounds, but we do hear the occasional rumble of a vehicle along some road bridge. Unconsciously & instinctively we remain silent.*

Greystones[1], 3rd of August, 1871[2], 1 AM

⇥ 2 ⇤

## *'Pain & Bravery'*

*To have feeling but to lack its fit expression*
*To be dumb amid the music-world of life*
*To be still amid the roar & the progression*
*Where the worker as he touches stamps possession –*
*To be fettered by our hearts before the strife –*

---

[1]  Greystones was (and still is) accessible from Dublin by train. Today it is the southern terminus of the DART railway line.

[2]  Stoker rendered his dates numerically as day/month/year.

*To be crippled ere the race – to lose the Real*
*Which we erst have sadly toiled for and in vain*
*To seek among the passing forever our Ideal*
*This is pain.*

*To be hopeful looking towards a dull tomorrow*
*To be joyous when our dearest hopes have fled*
*To be strong of heart and mind amid our sorrow*
*And when night is closing darkly round to borrow*
*From the morning but a glimmer of its red*
*To be patient through all wrong and tribulation*
*And to trust Him who is mightier than the grave*
*This despite the coward cynic's protestation*
*Is to be brave.*

27<sup>th</sup> of October, 1872[3]

---

3    Although this is the first poem to appear in the Journal, it is not the
     first that Stoker wrote. 'Acrostic' was composed in 1870 and inserted
     later. See p. 48–9.

⊷ 3 ⊷

### 'Dreamland'[4]

*We have soared afar from sorrow: we have winged above the azure*
  *In a land away from warring we have fixed on our abodes;*
  *Here our troubles are forgotten, and we find a childish pleasure*
  *Building up our stately castles with our earthly borne loads.*

*Leave us, leave us friends that love us: we are happy in forgetting*
  *Let your pity never tear us from the thrones whereon we rest.*
  *Only think of us as happy. When the sun is brightly setting*
  *You may see our pleasant Dreamland in the clouds along the West.*

*Leave us in our golden palace in that happy Dreamland glowing*
  *Far away from woes and troubles in the land of nature's birth;*
  *Where the flowers are live with music and where zephyrs faintly blowing*

---

4    Dreams form a central motif in Stoker's first collection, *Under the Sunset*.

*Bear the strains of quiet gladness – whisper
echoes from the earth.*

*But alas! How frail our castles and our stately
mansions builded*
   *They are founded not on rock but are reared
upon the sand;*
   *And our Dreamland melts in shadow with the
joys wherewith we filled it*
   *By the voice of nature speaking or the touch of
human hand.*

26th of January, 1873

⇥ 4 ⇤

*One starry-looking cloud supported by a wind-
sweep resting passive in the pure azure as though
a breeze were frozen in its course.*

15th of June, 1874

⇥ 5 ⇤

*Why not put the sound of bells into a painted
landscape? Suppose by tremulous lines suggestive
of vibration sufficient to catch the eye unconsciously but no more & leading to or from the*

*object in connection with the bells such as a tower or spire.*

July, 1874

⇥ 6 ⇤

*A web-legged girl with legs like flippers of a seal.*[5]

⇥ 7 ⇤

*Story of man like musical instruments in turn. Now drone of oboe, now shriek of violin, now blare of trumpet.*

10<sup>th</sup> of January, 1874

---

5   In one of many poignant Irish legends of Selkies or Selchies, 'A girl and her betrothed were fishing one day off the coast of Ireland, when their small boat capsized. The young man made every effort to rescue the struggling lass. As she disappeared under the waves, she cried out that he would hear her singing to him, that she would come back as a white seal and haunt him. He searched the shore for her in vain, then one night from his bed, he heard singing, and rushed in the darkness towards the sea. In the morning the boy's body was found on the rocky shore, clasped in the embrace of a dead white seal.'

## 8

*I[6] have known some queer things in the way of vagaries of the human voice. I have been in the room when a great voiced orator was speaking & the voice rebounding from the opposite wall hit him in the head and it began to swell. Again a singer let out his voice in a large hall with a panelled ceiling & the voice got broken up & fell down on the floor jingling the broken glass. Again I saw a voice clinging up in a corner & had the wife out with a brush & the place cleansed with a strong pair of bellows. Again I saw a voice strike a nail and the singer stood too near the wall & it went round with desperate speed like a Catherine wheel[7] or a humming top & when it was struck, part of it flew up and buzzed amongst the rafters.*

## 9

*The hearth was bright & the kettle like a dying Phoenix singing on its fiery bed.*

---

6    When Bram uses the first person pronoun, he may – or may not – be referring to himself. In this case, the reference to a wife (which Bram would not acquire for a few more years) indicates that the persona is someone else, either real or imagined.

7    Named for St Catherine of Alexandria.

⊷═ 10 ═⊶

*Subject for an allegorical work*
*'Blackguards[8] pegging mud at a hearse'*

⊷═ 11 ═⊶

*'The modesty of ignorance'*

⊷═ 12 ═⊶

*'Invertebrate Professions'*

⊷═ 13 ═⊶

*For farce – An impulse a tergo[9] to be called 'hitting*
*in the wind'.*

⊷═ 14 ═⊶

*As we passed through the wood in the twilight*

---

8    Blackguard (pronounced 'blaggard'): a ne'er-do-well, a scoundrel.

9    A term that crops up frequently throughout the Journal, 'a tergo' is Latin for 'from behind' or 'the rear end'. Bram was not averse to occasional touches of off-colour humour.

*the gentle wind took the puffs of steam from the engine and carried them in tall columns till they looked like ghosts among the trees.*

3rd of April, 1875

═ 15 ═

*'Love at Play'*

*Love is not dead nor sleeping*
*The playful boy pretends to die*
*See – see he peeps with laughing eye*
*He tests the lover's truth with weeping.*

*Love is nought but lying*
*Its wiles are jest to earnest carried*
*When Cupid smiles on lovers married*
*The thought that troubles least is dying.*

*Lovers be happy toying*
*Still be children whilst ye may*
*Ye will be grave in coming day*
*Youth not age is the season for enjoying.*

24th of August, 1875

### ⊷ 16 ⊷

#### *Subject of Essay*

*The honour due to those who fail after almost succeeding or after long & patient struggles. It is simply by accident generally that the scale is turned in favour of the winner.*

### ⊷ 17 ⊷

*Short story. Man who sought perfection in every way but could never find it.*

### ⊷ 18 ⊷

*Andy, the driver of the car in Mountshannon[10] which we took every day to drive to Turkenagh Lodge[11] said that a deer used to come out of Mr Read's wood & eat his cabbage every night – & at last Mr Read gave him leave to catch him. Andy went on, 'An' so sorh I sot a clothesline between two*

---

10　A village in Co. Clare.

11　Turkenagh Lodge was a hunting lodge, the ruins of which survive today.

*threes wid a bit of a loop on it an' in the mornin'*
*shure there he was fast enough.'*
   *'And what did you do then Andy?'*
   *'Faath sorh. I shkinned him an' ate him.'*[12]

[Marg:[13] In 'The Snake's Pass' 1889]

---

12   See *The Snake's Pass*, p. 73. This is one of many examples of Stoker's rendering of local dialect.

13   Several marginalia appear throughout the Journal. This one, along with other references to *The Snake's Pass* and *Under the Sunset*, was added by Florence Stoker many years later.

⇒ 19 ⇐

### 'Never Alone'

Never alone since she is near me
Spirit to spirit in joyous air
My soul sings blythe and she seems to hear me
For nature smiles and all is fair
For nature smiles and all is fair
All is fair – all is fair – all – all – all is fair.

Sorrows may come but they cannot harm me
She is happy – away with care
Her musical laughter still can charm me
Memory singing and all is fair
Memory singing and all is fair
All is fair – all is fair – all – all – all is fair.

Never alone when she has sorrow
Then trouble and I drop tear on tear
The sun pales dim and the grave's tomorrow
Is all that is left me since all is drear
All that is left for all is drear
All is drear – all is drear – all – all – all is drear.

Never alone, though far asunder
And oceans between us forever roll
Sorrow may moan & trouble thunder

*Never alone, but soul to soul*
*Never alone, but soul to soul*
*Soul to soul – soul to soul – soul to soul – soul to soul.*

4<sup>th</sup> of November, 1874

⁓ 20 ⁓

*'Too Lightly Won'*

*So ends my dream. My life must be*
*One long regret and misery*
*Loved not, though loving, what care I*
*How soon I die.*
*For whilst I live my wail must ever run*
*Too lightly won! Too lightly won.*

*His heart when he was sad & lone*
*Beat like an echo to mine own*
*But when he knew I loved him well*
*His ardour fell.*
*Love ceased for him whene'er the strife was done*
*And I was won. Too lightly won.*

*Had I been fickle, false or cold*
*His love perchance I still might hold*
*Alas! To grieve for spoken truth*
*For blighted hope – for ruined youth*

*Oh life of woe and anguish soon begun*
*Alas! For love too lightly won – too lightly won.*

25th of January, 1874[14]

⊷ 21 ⊶

### Mem

*Write series of short stories 'Old Friends in New*
*Clothes' (?) old myths modernized.*
*    I. Venus, Mars & Vulcan. Vulcan an old iron-*
*master wealthy – lame etc. Venus young wife.*
*Mars officer quartered in the neighbourhood.*

⊷ 22 ⊶

### 'Mary' (1)

*A woman weeping, joyous and alone*
*Freed from the memory of that mighty stone*
*That lay o'er Lazarus in his cavern tomb;*
*Weeping such tears as those the Master shed*

---

14    This dating suggests that this poem had been written earlier and tran-
      scribed at a later time.

*When eager friends were pointing where the dead*
*Lay in corruption's solitary gloom.*

*Mourning her spoken words her tears she dried*
*'Hadst thou been here my brother had not died.'*
*And once again the tears rained ever faster.*
*'O ye of little faith.' 'I should have known*
*'The tender love whence sprung that spirit groan*
*'That wrung the bosom of the weeping Master.*

*'No word to me when at His feet I lay*
*'He spoke, but to the friends I heard him say,*
*'"Where have they laid him?" And my pain was o'er*
*'For oh that voice! Its very tone was rest*
*'The dead came forth – this weary heart was blest –*
*'Alas! But emptier than it was before.'*

8th of February, 1877

—= 23 =—

*'If I don't eat something soon my stomach will*
*think my throat is cut.'*

[Marg: In 'The Snake's Pass', 1889][15]

---

15    See *The Snake's Pass*, p. 140.

### 'Mary' (2)

*In the dark night the woman stood alone*
*Hard by the tomb that lacked the sealing stone*
*All deathly silent, ere the morn begin*
*She wept, and weeping looked within the tomb*
*And saw the cere-cloths shining mid the gloom*
*And angels' snowy raiment bright within.*

*'Why weep ye, woman?' asked the whiterobed pair*
*'That they have ta'en my Lord I know not where.'*
*And as she spake she turned in sad surprise*
*There stood the gardener who in strange voice said:*
*'Woman, why weepest thou?' Again she pled*
*'If thou hast ta'en Him tell me where He lies.'*

*And then, oh wonder! came a word and voice*
*That in an instant made her heart rejoice.*
*'Mary!' Her Lord himself behind her stood*
*She turned to Him her full heart beating faster*
*And at His feet she fell & whispered 'Master!'*
*God – heart & human felt that all was good.*

*Forth went her loving hands to touch His shoon*

*But He with warning sweet denied the boon*
*'Nay! Touch me not, for yet I must ascend.'*
*The eager hands drew back, she raised her eyes*
*Obedience glad to give – a new surprise –*
*Eyes. God's at once & man's upon her bend.*

*'Go', said the tender voice 'and tell each friend*
*I to my Father and to yours ascend*
*And to my God & to your God I go.'*
*'My God & His! And we again shall meet*
*And He shall raise me weeping from His feet*
*Before our Father's eyes – The eyes I know!'*

25<sup>th</sup> of March, 1877

## 25

### *'Immoral Essays'*[16]

I. *A Defence of Hypocrisy*

II. *A Plea for Cannibalism*

III. *The Pleasure and Profit of being in debt*[17]

---

16  Here and elsewhere, Stoker appears to be imitating Leitch Ritchie, who in *Friendship's Offering* (1844), plays with a similar set of juxtaposed virtues and vices.

17  Beginning with III, somebody (likely Florence Stoker) has written over the faint originals in a different hand.

⇥ 26 ⇤

*The waiter said, 'Ah sir, get married. You never knew what happiness is till you've a wife. An' shure if ye haven't a wife ye grow old an' ye grow rich an' them does be round you that don't care for ye but only want yer money. An' sir, they do be only helpin' God away with ye.'*

[Marg: In 'The Snake's Pass' 1889][18]

⇥ 27 ⇤

*The name of the Farce oftenest played in the Real Life Theatre is 'Promised Another, or Don't you wish you may get her.'*

---

18    See *The Snake's Pass*, pp. 83–4.

— 28 —

*'The cryptic meaning of silence'*

— 29 —

**'The Wiles of Woman'**

*I was standing before the hotel door (Co. Limerick) smoking a cigarette after dinner. An ill-dressed man with a shadowy coat & no shirt & a short stick under his arm came up. He evidently wanted someone to talk to so he stopped & looked round for some object to serve as a topic of conversation. In the doorway of the next house was a handsome servant girl.*

*'That's a fine lookin' girl, sir', he spoke with the broadest of Limerick brogues – the sound of which is peculiar, each word begins high & the voice drops at the end of it.*

*'Yes she is', said I.*

*'Oh the wemen the wemen the wemen the wemen the wemen. God placed them on the airth to be a help to man – an' they're not that.'*

*'How do you make that out?'*

*'Well, sir, ye see that if a man looks twice at a good lookin' girl the first thing she axes him to do is to write her a letther. An' then she has him. For when a man goes to write a letther to a girl he can't, if he's a man at all at all, begin with less than a "my dear" – or even "my darling" an' then she has him again. An' then you do be brought into the Coort and ye do be frowned at be the judge an' ye do be badgered be the counsellors an' ye do have to pay yer money – an' there ye are.'*

[Marg: Snake's Pass 1890][19]

⊷═ 30 ═⊷

*He also told me a harrowing tale of a woman who had married a wealthy grocer of the town by means of an action for breach of promise. 'He found it would be cheaper to marry her nor to pay her – an' sorr', added my ragged friend, 'what do ye think, she was no more now a mere simple governess.'*

[Marg: Snake's Pass 1889]

---

19    See *The Snake's Pass*, p. 82.

⤙ **31** ⤚

*Mem for story*

*A man builds up a shadow on a wall bit by bit by adding to substance. Suddenly the shadow becomes alive.*

[Marg: Idea used in Under the Sunset]

⤙ **32** ⤚

*Mem for story in 'Under the Sunset'*

*'The King of the Spiders'*[20]

---

20   There is no story of that title in the collection. Stoker might have had in
     mind Charles Dickens's *Dirty Old Man* (aka *The King of Spiders*), 1852.

## ⤙ 33 ⤚

### *Mem for story*

*A man writes a play. Actor of chief part gets sick. Plays part himself. Girl in female part just suitable. Acting is reality. Carries away audience – high hopes – but next night freshness gone – playing dull & play hissed.*

## ⤙ 34 ⤚

*Subject for character comedietta 'Uncle Toby's Courtship'. Characters Toby, Widow Widman, Trim, Bridget.*[21]

## ⤙ 35 ⤚

### *Mem Story for children*

*Palace of Fairy Queen. Child goes to sleep & palace grows – sky changes into blue silk curtains etc.*

---

21    Apparently, Stoker was toying with the idea of a variation/adaptation of Laurence Sterne's 'Uncle Toby's Courtship' from *Tristram Shandy*, vol. 6, 1759.

### ↠ 36 ↞

*'The Responsibility of Doubt'*

### ↠ 37 ↞

*Said the Jarvie[22] to me 3.1.78. 'Sir there's some terrible disorther intirely amongst horse cattle these times. They do be dyin' from aff iv our hands just for all the world like rotten sheep[23] an' no man can tell what ails them at all at all.[24] There's misther Docther Professional Ferguson himself (Prof. Ferguson) an' he can't get undher it.'*

[Marg: In The Snake's Pass 1889][25]

---

22  A 'jarvie' is the driver of a horse-drawn hackney coach (cab).

23  The reference is to liver-rot and foot-rot, conditions that resulted from the wetness of the soil.

24  During the 1870s, people still held to the view that plagues were of spontaneous origin. Sick animals were not culled, and veterinarians were powerless to treat the disease.

25  See *The Snake's Pass*, p. 30.

## 38

### 'Mary' (3)

*In Martha's house the weary Master lay*
*Spent with His faring through the burning day*
*The busy hostess bustled through the room*
*On household cares intent, and at His feet*
*The gentle Mary took her wonted seat*
*Soft came His voice like music through the gloom.*

*Cumbered about much serving Martha wrought –*
*Her sister listening as the Master taught –*
*Till vexed and fretful an appeal she made*
*'Doth it not matter that on me doth fall*
*The burden? Mary helpeth not at all.*
*Master! Command her that she give me aid.'*

*'Ah Martha, Martha, thou art full of care*
*And many things thy needless trouble share.'*
*Thus with the love that chides the master spake*
*'One thing alone is needful. That good part*
*Hath Mary chosen from her loving heart.*
*And that part from her I shall never take.'*

*One thing alone we lack: our souls indeed*
*Have fiercer hunger than the body's need*
*Ah! happy they that look in loving eyes.*
*The harsh world round them fades; the Master's voice*
*In sweetest music bids their souls rejoice*
*And wakes an echo there that never dies.*

14th of November, 1878 [Marg: In 'The Youth's Companion'
Boston Mass USA]26

⊷ 39 ⊷

*Memo for new Children's Book*27
*The man who bought pains [deleted – 'written']*
*The Coming Man*
*The Mosaic of Life*

4th of August, 1881

---

26   This poem was published with minor revisions as 'One Thing Needful'
     in *The Youth's Companion* (10 December 1885, vol. 58, p. 522). Curiously,
     an advertisement for *The Youth's Companion* (in *The Quiver*, December
     1885) announces among its contents 'Lord Tennyson Among his
     Familiars', an illustrated sketch by Bram Stoker. To date we have been
     unsuccessful in tracking this down.

27   This new book never materialised.

⊷ 40 ⊶

## *Mem*

*Story 'The Musical Liar' – lying in musical phrases*

⊷ 41 ⊶

## *Mem*

*Story 'The Angry Waters' wishes ill to person &
kills then murmurs on sorrowfully for ever.*

[written][28]

⊷ 42 ⊶

## *Mem*

*Immoral essays
The pleasure and profit of being in debt. See p. 110[29]*

---

28    Likely a reference to *The Watter's Mou'* published in 1894: 'The waves still
       beat into the Watter's Mou' with violence, for though the storm had
       passed. The sea was a wide-stretching mass of angry waters…' (p. 21).

29    Stoker is reminding himself of an earlier entry.

## ⋆⋙ 43 ⋘⋆

### *Mem*

*Irish story Torriadbreena. Shifting bog – William (Haggerty) makes good man exchange his land which lies lower down from bog above in hopes of finding buried treasure. Bog shifts & good man finds iron chest of money in cleft of rock laid bare – christens good man's daughter – poet & natural – young engineer who comes to find treasure by magnets etc – gombeen man[30] – priest etc.*

2<sup>nd</sup> of November, 1881 [Marg: Written 'The Snake's Pass' 1889[31]]

## ⋆⋙ 44 ⋘⋆

### *'Mary' (4)*

*Of man's full stature, fresh from stainless youth
Strong from repression, sweet with cultured ruth –*

---

30   'Gombeen man' is a pejorative term used in Ireland for a moneylender, a shady small-time wheeler-dealer.

31   *The Snake's Pass* was not published until 1890. However, an excerpt entitled 'The Gombeen Man' (Chapter 3 of the novel) appeared in *The People* in 1889.

*In all things even as his fellows were*
*The Master, conscious of a good man's power*
*Went on his way at the appointed hour*
*The loving message of his God to bear.*

*Through doubt and danger – friends deterrent fears*
*Through peoples savage with the hate of years –*
*With holy insight and a purpose deep*
*To give God glory and the son of God*
*To hostile Juda on his way he trod*
*There to awaken Lazarus from sleep.*

*Through the long journey how His great heart beat*
*Full of the promise of a meeting sweet*
*When tears should cease and loving eyes be dried*
*Then by the way he paused and Martha came*
*And half in reverence spake, and half in blame*
*'Hadst Thou been here, my brother had not died.'*

*Was nothing lacking in the spoken word*
*That never echo in this spirit stirred?*
*Was accent loveless or too full of blame?*
*Or – in the loving heart was naught of pain*
*That of His friend the dead man's sister's twain*
*Forth from the household but one sister came?*

*Else what saw Martha in those eyes serene?*
*What the dim hope from woman's instinct keen*
*As home she turned in secret haste to flee?*
*Still mid the loving friends that mourned the dead*
*Her sister Mary bowed her patient head –*
*'The Master! He has come and calleth thee!'*

*Struggling she rose, they too that vigil kept*
*She seeks the grave – not all her tears are wept*
*In true friend's comfort ever tears are dried –*
*But Mary sank before the master's feet*
*And to him murmured in her accents sweet*
*'Hadst thou been here my brother had not died.'*

*What then the trouble of His noble breast*
*Who erst had patience for His God's behest –*
*Who thither went to raise the dead that slept?*
*Sad thoughts of vigil – long expected aid*
*Of pure love doubting of the hopes it made*
*God knoweth all our secrets – Jesus wept.*

⇥ 45 ⇤

### *Mem subject for story*

*Man married by proxy – is already married.*
*Proxy married without knowing it?*

## ⟿ 46 ⟾

### *Mem – story*

*Go to sleep under rug of cat skins.*

31<sup>st</sup> of August, 1875

## ⟿ 47 ⟾

### *Mem – story*

*Seaport. Two sailors love girl – one marries her, other swears revenge. Husband goes out to sea soon after marriage & on return after some days sees in grey light of morning his young wife crucified on the great cross which stands at end of pier.*

## ⟿ 48 ⟾

### *Mem*

*Love – a serpent coiled round the heart – the influence of the presence of the one loved on it & on her or him.*

⚬ **49** ⚬

*Mem – story*

*Young man amongst old clerks.*

⚬ **50** ⚬

*Mem – story*

*One sends letter in wrong envelope on purpose to create false impression.*

⚬ **51** ⚬

*Mem for story 'The Death Eels of the Wey'*[32]

⚬ **52** ⚬

*Mem for story*

*Husband goes to Gipsies & learns that he will murder his wife. She goes also to quiet him & asks*

---

32 The River Wey, in Surrey, passes through the town of Godalming before flowing into the Thames.

*her fortune. Is told that she will be murdered by*
*her husband.*

7<sup>th</sup> **of September, 1872** [Marg: written 'A Gipsy Prophecy'[33]
in the New York Christmas 'Spirit of the Times']

⇥ 53 ⇤

*'Acrostic'*[34]

*Before we met I had not thought of love*
*Except in poems where it rhymes with dove*
*Sent down for metre's sake from realms above*
*So slept my life away – I little thought*
*I should awake to what I dreamed was nought*
*Except a flying vision fancy fraught*
*L'amour la gloir le rien is now my prayer*
*Entranced by love, now glory bids me dare*
*Supreme I rise by wine above despair*
*To me the love exists I feel it here*
*Return my passion banish every fear*

---

33   'A Gipsy Prophecy' also appeared in the collection *Dracula's Guest and*
     *Other Weird Stories* (1914).

34   Other well-known examples of acrostics include 'An Acrostic' by Poe
     and 'A Boat Beneath a Sunny Sky' by Lewis Carroll.

*And glory shall be mine when thou art near*
*No care I dread the wine of hope shall lend*
*Good cheer that I may suffer to the end*
*Entombing love within the sepulchre of friend.*

AS 3rd of March, 1870[35]

---

35     This makes it his earliest extant poem. The sheet was inserted into the
pages of the Journal at a later date.

A web-legged girl - with legs like flippers a seal.

Subject for drama Poe's "Fall of the House of Usher
25/10/72

Story of man who reflects everybody's self who meets him. 1/10/73

Story of man brought to life in a dissecting room & the application of a new power unexpected.

tuation. H.B.P. sketching behind the Buck stone, forest of & pic nic behind the stone. Girl sings "when the Dove" he answers with "Ruddier than the Cherry" asked to join &c

# TWO

# ⇒ EN ROUTE ⇐ TO *DRACULA*

The final dated entry in the Journal was made in June 1882, eight years before Bram Stoker began his notes for his novel *Dracula*. Yet he may have had some of the entries in mind (or even at his side) while he was composing his masterpiece. Several entries have distinct resonances in *Dracula*, indicating that the Journal should be looked at as one of the breeding grounds for his most famous book.

Making entries in his Journal helped Stoker hone his writing skills in very tangible ways. Much of what he wrote is a series of reminders, items that he feared might otherwise be forgotten in the busy schedule that was his life. The reminders were, of course, to himself. One doubts he had any intention of sharing the Journal with anybody else (though as stated earlier, his wife Florence, who survived him for twenty-five years, read it at some point and made marginal notes). Sometimes he even highlighted his aide-memoires with the designation 'Mem':

Mem Write poor Duff's funeral
Mem Write series of short stories
Mem – story. Go to sleep under rug of cat skins

The astute reader of *Dracula* will immediately recognise the technique, recalling similar notations made by Jonathan Harker – himself a compulsive note-taker. His journal is punctuated with memos. As he records his meal of chicken at the hotel in Klausenburgh, he hastily adds in parentheses: '*Mem*., get recipe for Mina' (*Dracula*, p. 1). As he travels deeper into Transylvania and recalls how he has read of this region as a centre of superstitions, he jots down (again parenthetically) '*Mem*., I must ask the Count all about them' (p. 2). As he records an all-night conversation with the Count at Castle Dracula, Harker makes this observation: '*Mem*., this diary seems horribly like the beginning of the "Arabian Nights", for everything has to break off at cock-crow – or like the ghost of Hamlet's father' (p. 31). The compulsion to 'write it down' is strong. Harker, recording in his journal a conversation with Dracula, notes, 'I wish I could put down all he said exactly as he said it' (p. 29). Later, in a desperate attempt to cope with the reality of his encounter with the three female vampires, Harker, echoing Hamlet, exclaims, 'My tablets! Quick, my tablets!/'Tis meet that I put it down' (p. 37).

*William Rider edition, 1912*

Bram Stoker's ever handy 'pocket-book' along with this Journal answers a question so often raised: how much does Stoker's work, in particular *Dracula*, reflect the life and essence of its author? Here we see a clear parallel between the young travelling solicitor (Jonathan Harker) and the young travelling clerk of the court (Bram Stoker) who would in time be called to the Bar.

Harker is not the only character in *Dracula* who habitually keeps notes. Mina, in a letter to Lucy, makes this declaration:

> I shall keep a diary … a sort of journal which I can write in whenever I feel inclined. I do not suppose there will be much of interest to other people; but it is not intended for them … It is really an exercise book. I shall try to do what I see lady journalists do: interviewing and writing descriptions and trying to remember conversations. I am told that, with a little practice, one can remember all that goes on or that one hears said during a day. (p. 55)

Through the course of the narrative, Mina supplies Van Helsing with important notes that she has kept. At one point she produces a lengthy memorandum outlining various means of attack (pp. 361–3). Her notes help ensure that Dracula will be tracked down and destroyed.

Dr John Seward records his diary on phonograph: 'Let me put down with exactness all that happened … Not a detail that I can recall must be forgotten' (p. 282).

Lucy, at her death, leaves a memorandum. Even the lunatic Renfield 'keeps a little note-book in which he is always jotting down something' (p. 71). In fact, the entire novel is a patchwork of notes of various kinds: journal entries, diary entries, letters, memoranda, phonograph recordings, telegrams, newspaper reports and a ship's log. *Dracula* is the story of the production of a text. Its narrators (of whom there are several) can record only what they have experienced individually, and the text provides no omniscient voice. Furthermore, the process of preservation and transmission of the various pieces that comprise the text utilises many forms: notes kept in shorthand, recorded on gramophones, transcribed (in duplicate) by typewriter and sent by telegraph. Stoker draws on up-to-date technology, having his characters take advantage of means of communication not available to him as note-keeper in the 1870s.

Another device employed throughout the Journal is the recreation of local dialect. Stoker attempts to represent local speech: for example 'threes' for 'trees' and 'sorh' for 'sir'. He incorporates some of his results into *The Snake's Pass*, his Irish novel. Here Stoker was working with the familiar, close enough to the scene to be able to 'hear' the idiom, speech pattern, accent and lilt as he wrote. Even though recreation of dialect can create problems for the reader, the technique adds to a story's realism. It was a skill that Stoker would further develop during his years with the theatre, acquiring an ear for the sounds of dialects in stage scripts.

The representation of dialect in *Dracula* was more of a challenge. Here is a sample:

It be all fool-talk, lock, stock, and barrel; that's what it be an' nowt else. These bans an' wafts an' boh-ghosts an' bar-guests an' bogles an' all anent them is only fit to set bairns an' dizzy women a'belderin'. They be nowt but air-blebs. They, an' all grims an' signs an' warnin's, be all invented by parsons an' illsome berk-bodies an' railway touters to skeer an' scunner hafflin's, an' to get folks to do somethin' that they don't other incline to. It makes me ireful to think o' them. Why, it's them that, not content with printin' lies on paper an' preachin' them out of pulpits, does want to be cuttin' them on the tombsteans. Look here all around you in what airt ye will. All them steans, holdin' up their heads as well as they can out of their pride, is acant – simply tumblin' down with the weight o' the lies wrote on them. (*Dracula*, pp. 66-7)

Here the dialect is that of Whitby, a town on the Yorkshire coast of England that he visited during the summer of 1890. He made a concerted effort to achieve accuracy, having gained access to a very useful book:

*A Whitby Glossary* (1876) by F. K. Robinson. From it he took four pages of notes for *Dracula*, listing local-isms followed by standard meanings. He assiduously worked many of these into the comments made by Mr Swales in Chapter 6 of the novel.

*A page from Stoker's Notes for Dracula. Stoker gathered a list of localisms for his recreation of the Whitby dialect.*

As for subject matter, there are no references to vampires in the Journal. However, we do find early indications of Bram's interest in the Gothic literary tradition. There are allusions to Edgar Allan Poe (54, 56) including a sugges-tion about dramatising 'The Fall of the House of Usher'. Worthy of note is the fact that Bram may have changed the original ending of his novel (in which the castle is destroyed by a cataclysmic event) because it was too similar to the ending of Poe's famous short story.

Gothic elements are prevalent in his early fiction published while he was keeping his Journal. Even though the themes of death, darkness and decay are grounded in realism (alcoholism and family violence), a developing Gothicism is evident. Allusions to *Faust* are prominent, a significant foreshadowing of the impact of that legend on *Dracula*. In 'The Chain of Destiny', the author utilises the Gothic tropes of an old ancestral home, a portrait, an ancient curse and nightmares.

The closest we get to vampires in the Journal are the references to Dion Boucicault. We know that Stoker was acquainted with Boucicault (see Chapter 7) and most likely was familiar with his popular play *The Vampire: A Phantom Related in Three Dramas* (1852), with its vampire – Sir Alan Raby – clearly descended from John Polidori's 'The Vampyre' (1819). His association with Boucicault, almost twenty years before he began working on *Dracula*, may have planted an early seed.

Specific images and motifs among the Journal entries crop up in some form in *Dracula*. The boy with the flies imprisoned in a bottle (55) foreshadows Renfield's habit of collecting (and eventually eating) flies. The man who reflects everybody's self who meets him (57) is an early allusion to a central motif in *Dracula*, that the non-human vampire casts no reflection.

An even more intriguing link can be found in 'Mem for story: The Quatorzième' (63). A 'quatorzième' (from the French for 'fourteenth') is a professional guest whose function is to be the fourteenth person at a dinner party for thirteen. The intention was to counteract the bad luck associated with the number thirteen, which many in Christian cultures trace back to the fact that there were thirteen attendees at Christ's Last Supper, including the one who would betray him. Bram was at some point planning to build a story around this concept. He did not write it. But he did write something similar – in his notes for *Dracula*. At an early stage, he had planned for Seward (at that point unnamed) to hold a dinner party:

> The dinner party at the mad doctor's – thirteen
> Thirteen – each has a number
> Each asked to tell something strange – order of numbers makes the story complete
> At the end the Count comes in. (*Bram Stoker's Notes for Dracula*, p. 23)

The Count is the quatorzième. A nifty touch! On a list of characters made shortly afterwards, Stoker refines this, making a notation ('mem: makes dinner of 13'). The list of characters not deleted at that point totalled thirteen, including the Count. A Last Supper with the anti-Christ! None of this found its way into the novel, but it is interesting that the idea of the quatorzième resurfaced in this way.

Bram Stoker, though predominantly an 'arts' person, had a keen interest in science and related fields (such as medicine). In fact, three of his brothers were medical doctors. Two intriguing entries in the Journal refer to contemporary scientific (and/or pseudo-scientific) fields. That he was fascinated by both is evident in the following comment that he made in 1901 in the Preface to the Icelandic edition of Dracula: 'I am further convinced that they must always remain to some extent incomprehensible, although continuing research in psychology and natural sciences may, in years to come, give logical explanations of such strange happenings which at present, neither scientists nor the secret police can understand' ('Author's Preface', p. 278).

One such topic appears on a page of the Journal that contains only a heading: 'Electrobiology' (61). Electrobiology is the study of electrical activity in living organisms. In the nineteenth century, many pseudo-scientists made a connection between electrical impulses and hypnotism, mesmerism and the pre-hypnotic state of catalepsy. One such individual was John Jones, author of *The Natural and the Supernatural: or, Man – Physical, Apparitional and Spiritual* (1861). This book is on the list of source texts that Stoker consulted during his research for *Dracula*. In the novel, Van Helsing observes as follows: 'Let me tell you, my friend, that there are things done today in electrical science which would have been deemed unholy by the very men who discovered electricity' (p. 195). Later in the book, Stoker expands electrical phenomena to include the geologic and chemical attributes:

> The very place … is full of strangeness of the geologic and chemical world. There are deep caverns and fissures that reach none know whither. There have been volcanoes, some of whose openings still send out waters of strange properties … Doubtless there is something magnetic or electric in some of these combinations of occult forces which work for physical life in strange way. (*Dracula*, p. 329)

Though Stoker changed the ending, resonances of his original intention (to have Castle Dracula destroyed in a volcanic eruption) linger.

The case for 'Physiognomony' (62) is much more pronounced. Bram refers to it in a letter to Walt Whitman sent in 1876, just months before the Journal entry:

> I know you from your works and your photograph, and if I know anything about you I think you would like to know

of the personal appearance of your correspondents. You are I know a keen physiognomist. I am a believer of the science myself and am in an humble way a practicer of it.

Physiognomy is the assessment of a person's character and personality from their outward physical appearance. Popular in the nineteenth century, its major proponent was J. C. Lavater in *Essays on Physiognomy* (5 vols). Bram Stoker possessed a copy of Lavater's work. As to whether or not Bram was indeed a 'practicer' of it – it is certainly a factor in many of his books, most notably *Dracula*.

1.  Mina's description of Van Helsing:
    The poise of the head strikes one at once as indicative of thought and power; the head is noble, well-sized, broad, and large behind the ears. The face, clean-shaven, shows a hard, square chin, a large resolute, mobile mouth, a good-sized nose, rather straight, but with quick, sensitive nostrils, that seem to broaden as the big, bushy brows come down and the mouth tightens. The forehead is broad and fine, rising at first almost straight and then sloping back above two bumps or ridges wide apart; such a forehead that the reddish hair cannot possibly tumble over it, but falls naturally back and to the sides. (p. 185)

2. Lucy's Description of Dr Seward:

   I told you of him … with the strong jaw and the good forehead. (p. 58)

3. Jonathan's description of Count Dracula:

   His face was a strong – a very strong – aquiline, with high bridge of the thin nose and peculiarly arched nostrils; with lofty domed forehead, and hair growing scantily round the temples, but profusely elsewhere. His eyebrows were very massive, almost meeting over the nose … The mouth was fixed and rather cruel-looking … his ears were pale and at the tops extremely pointed; the chin was broad and strong, and the cheeks firm though thin. (p. 18)

The description of the Count echoes several physical features outlined by physiognomist Cesare Lombroso in *Criminal Man* (1895). We know that Stoker was familiar with Lombroso, as he mentions him by name in *Dracula* (p. 352).

Stoker maintained this propensity to connect physiology and character long after the publication of *Dracula*. For example, he interviewed Winston Churchill in 1908, and described him as follows:

The red hair of his boyhood has now lost some of its fire, and seems now rather a reddish brown than red. The eyes of light blue are large of pupil having in them something of the free quality of the eyes of a bird. The mouth is an orator's mouth; clear cut, expressionable, and not small. The forehead is both broad and high, with a fairly deep vertical line above the nose; the chin strong and well formed. His hands are somewhat remarkable: a sort of index to his life as well as to his general character. They are distinctly strong hands. Broad in the palm, with that breadth which palmists take as showing honesty; fingers both long and fairly thick, but tapering; the thumb slightly bent backward at the top joint. The man with such a hand should go far. (Stoker, 'Mr Winston Churchill', p. 125)

Yet another intriguing Journal entry is the 'Story of man brought back to life in a dissecting room by the application of a new power unexpected' (58). Though the resonance here is more of *Frankenstein* (Mary Shelley, 1818), a similar motif made its way into Stoker's *Dracula* Notes. In what had been originally intended as the opening chapter (later discarded), Harker describes the Count as 'old dead man made alive' (*Bram Stoker's Notes for Dracula*, p. 17). In a visit to the Dead House in Munich (another segment dropped from the final MS) Harker notes that he 'Saw old man on bier ...

return on inquiry and find corpse gone' (*Notes for Dracula*, p. 35).

The Journal breathes new life into *Dracula*, offering fresh insights into Stoker's method of composition as well as motifs for his plot and characters.

## TRANSCRIPTIONS

### ⇒ 54 ⇐

*At the Penny Reading in the School House Greystones tonight, Mr Jones a local genius read the Raven.*[36] *He is a big man with immense hands and feet. He only succeeded in making the audience laugh consumedly but to me the effect was painful. A man who genuinely felt in his soul every word he uttered and yet unable from want of education to do more than cause a laugh. Alas!*

13th of August, 1872

---

36   Famous poem by Edgar Allan Poe.

### ⇥ 55 ⇤

*'A Damned Lie'*

*I once knew a little boy who put so many flies into a bottle that they had not room to die!!!*

27th of October, 1872

### ⇥ 56 ⇤

*Subject for drama Poe's 'Fall of the House of Usher'*

25th of October, 1872

### ⇥ 57 ⇤

*Story of man who reflects everybody's self who meets him*

1st of October, 1873

### ⇥ 58 ⇤

*Story of man brought to life in a dissecting room by the application of a new power unexpected*

⟶ **59** ⟵

*Centrifugal & Centripetal People*

⟶ **60** ⟵

*Centrifugal & Centripetal*[37] *mem etc.*

*There are in nature two forces which affect moving bodies, one a centripetal force which impels towards some central point, the other a centrifugal force with an opposite tendency.*

*As all the things which exist move either by volition or in the ordinary scheme of things so are they ever influenced by one or other of these two forces unless indeed they fly ever in a circle.*

*As we see the various forces of nature typified in greater or less degree in different men so do we see these two forces amongst them, oftentimes to such degree as to eclipse all other manifest forces and as to seem to stand alone.*

*Thus there are those round whom as nucleus all things seem to gather – and those from whom all things seem to flee.*

---

37   Dr Seward uses these two terms opaquely in reference to his mental patient, R. M. Renfield (see *Dracula*, p. 81).

*analyse*
*magnet, repellent etc*
*spendthrift*
*selfish man*
*inquisitiveness*
*centres*
*complete circles*

18th of September, 1875

⇥ 61 ⇤

*Electrobiology*

⇥ 62 ⇤

*'Physiognomony'*[38]

*The two men were sitting over the rail of the milk cart. The two hawkers hurried up to get a lift. As they drew near, one of them a stout elderly woman called out. 'Shure an' it's the clever woman I am – with the fine eyesight intirely. I seen yez far*

---

38   'The science that reads in man's face the hidden secrets of his soul' (Mariano Aguirre de Venero, *New System of Physiognomony*, 1865).

*away an' I recognised your rump & Billy's an' yer old hat.'*

## ⇥ 63 ⇤

*Mem for story:*

*'The Quatorzième' – death coming on to 13 guests – making the 14th.*

27th of November, 1881

N. M. Woodroffe told me today (21.3.11) the following:

"An Irishman (Labourer) applied for a job. The employer not accepting him as skilled in any way asked:

"What can you do: what kind of work:

"I can do any kind of worruk!"

"Can you make a venetian blind?"

"I can aisy!"

De employer doubtful "Now how would you do it?"

Slower - confident, "Begob I'd give him a poke in th[e]

# THREE

# ⇒ HUMOUR ⇐

The Journal provides insight into Stoker as a developing writer. But it also reveals – in spades – an aspect of the author of *Dracula* that is frequently overlooked or at best, downplayed: his remarkable sense of humour. Scholars have for the most part bypassed this trait, content to psychoanalyse both the author and his characters, endlessly debating hidden sexual meanings in both his writing and his lifelong friendships. The revelations that this Journal provides should encourage a reassessment of the view of Stoker as an uptight, generally humourless individual.

Humour, defined as 'a contemplation of the incongruities of life', is usually occasioned by the juxtaposition of the ordinary and the unexpected: the Dean who joined the wrong people into holy matrimony (71), the doctor who claimed he could 'hear' better with an opera glass (131) and the Scotsman in full Highland dress who blew his nose into his napkin (106). Such situations generate laughter because each contains an element of surprise that clashes with the normalcy of the occasion. Stoker himself defined humour as having three components: 'exaggeration, incongruity and contrast' (69). All three elements manifest themselves throughout the Journal.

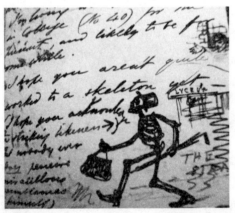

*A skeletal sketch of the hard-working Bram by William Fitzgerald, the artist who contributed several of the illustrations for* Under the Sunset

Clearly, Bram Stoker possessed a keen sense of the comic, and excelled at recognising incongruities around him and transmitting them to others in the form of both spoken and written narrative. First and foremost is the man himself. He enjoyed a good laugh and raised laughter among those around him. He was always a welcome speaker at dinner parties both in Dublin and (later) in London. 'He had a laugh that was good to hear', noted Henry Dickens (son of Charles).

His reputation as a raconteur with a comic bent spread widely once he left Dublin. During the 1880s when Stoker was gainfully employed as business manager for Henry Irving, the most successful actor of the Victorian stage, his sense of humour came in quite handy. Irving took Fussie (his fox terrier dog) on just about all his Lyceum Theatre Company tours, including seven of the eight to North America. Most American hotels banned dogs. Every time he was confronted with such a refusal, Irving would walk out. On one occasion in Detroit, permission for Fussie to stay was granted when Stoker intervened to point out to the hotel manager that his establishment already admitted animals – it was overrun with rats!

Stoker was not averse to having a bit of fun, even at his own expense. In his biography *A Strange Eventful History*, Michael Holroyd records that during a winter visit to Toronto with Irving in 1884, Stoker ventured into the world of tobogganing with somewhat predict-able results: 'Ellen [Terry] decided to go tobogganing: Henry stood in the snow, watching her with a curiously forlorn expression. And behind him Stoker had positioned himself, hesitating between trepidation and desire until, unable to resist the iced toboggan chutes, he leapt forward, fell off the toboggan, and went somersaulting down the hillside, flapping his arms' (p. 167).

The *St Paul Globe* (11 June 1900) recorded this account of Stoker's combination of humour and acumen:

Sir Henry Irving is known to be a very generous man, and would be robbed right and left, it is said, if it were not for the protection afforded by his business manager, Mr Bram Stoker. For instance, says a London correspondent of the St Louis *Globe-Democrat*, Irving recently received a letter from a man in Paris who told of his marked likeness to the great actor. At first, the stranger wrote, it was a pleasure to be taken for so distinguished a man, but in time the novelty wore off, and he had been both annoyed and embarrassed by the continual necessity of explaining that he was he, and not Sir Henry. The letter concluded by mentioning that £5 or £10 would be of considerable service to him. Would Sir Henry remit by return of post, and thus in a measure atone for the annoyance to which the likeness had subjected him?

Irving happened to read the letter to Bram Stoker, and then said that he thought he must send the man something, not £10 perhaps, but—'If ye'll let me, I'll answer the letter for you', said Mr Stoker, who has an Irish accent to match his Irish wit.

A few days later Irving said: 'You answered that letter, Mr Stoker?' 'I did, then, and wrote him advice of a friendly nature, besides the money I sent to him.' 'You sent him money, ha! I hope it was enough –' ' 'Twas, then', murmured Stoker, beaming, 'and the letter to boot. Shall I tell you what was in it? Well, then, it was half a crown I sent to him' – half a crown is 62 cents – 'and I just wrote him that since it was his likeness to you was vexin' him, well, then, to take it and go and have his hair cut.'

One of Stoker's best known stories, the tale of the christening (137) was adopted in a much shorter version by American humourist Mark Twain, a long-time friend, who included it in his repertoire. In fact, Stoker was once in the audience when Twain told it (*New York Tribune* 23 April 1891). Twain was still telling the story almost twenty years later (see *New York Times* 15 May 1908).

According to grand-nephew Daniel Farson, after Bram had moved to London, his wife Florence invited Mark Twain (Samuel Clemens) to tea:

Having given her maid instructions to admit nobody else, she waited – and waited. Finally she summoned the maid to inquire whether there had been any word.

'Oh no, Mum', said the maid.

'I thought I heard the doorbell.'

'Yes, Mum. That was a Mr Clemens but I told him you weren't at home.' (*The Man Who Wrote* Dracula, p. 112)

Bram had a special fondness for verbal humour and more sophisticated witticisms. Scattered throughout the Journal are riddles and word games. The Journal serves as a collection plate for Bram Stoker's bons mots, perhaps somewhat for his own amusement, but also to groom and shape for later use, and to sharpen his skills as a speaker and public figure. It should therefore come as little surprise that his published writings contain a preponderance of humour, sometimes obvious, sometimes more nuanced. Stoker scholar Carol A. Senf tells of a comic episode in 'The Man from Shorrox':

A poor Irish widow outsmarts a cocky Manchester businessman who had insisted on being put up in the best room in the hotel. After getting him drunk, she puts him in that room without revealing that its current occupant is a corpse. When he wakes up, he screams at discovering two people in the room, the watcher from the undertaker's and his girlfriend. His screams awaken everyone in the hotel, many of them already in on the joke.

Humour is also a prominent trait in many of the stories that comprise *Snowbound: The Record of a Theatrical Touring Party*, which editor Bruce Wightman describes as 'semi-factual', adding that many of the characters are 'disguised portraits of those theatricals the author worked and toured with' (p. 9). In 'A Lesson in Pets', Stoker presents a long-suffering manager (named Mr Benville Nonplusser) of a troupe of actors who insist on taking their pets on the road. After describing a veritable cacophony of 'barking and yelping and howling', the manager decides to take matters into his own hands by asking an animal importer for 'some sort of pet that wouldn't be pleasant for a nervous person to travel with' (p. 24). The answer is 'three ton of boa-constrictor from Surinam' (p. 25). Upon seeing the snakes, the other members of the troupe agree that no one should be allowed to take their pets on tour.

*Personal Reminiscences of Henry Irving*, Stoker's account of his years as Irving's theatre manager, is a treasure trove of humourous anecdotes which he took delight in sharing with his own readers. Here is one example:

[Henry VIII] ends with the christening of the infant Princess Elizabeth, in which of course a dummy baby was used ... When the play had run some forty nights Irving got a letter from which I quote: 'The complete success of Henry VIII was marred when the King kissed the china doll. The whole house tittered. Herewith I offer the hire of our real baby...' To this I replied:

'Mr Irving fears that there might be some difficulty in making the changes which you suggest ... A series of difficulties then arises, any of which you and your family might find insuperable. If your real baby were provided, it might be difficult, or even impossible, for the actor who impersonates King Henry VIII to feel the real feelings of a father towards it. This would necessitate your playing the part of the King, and further would require that your wife should play the part of Queen Anne Boleyn. This might not suit either of you – especially as in reality Henry VIII had afterwards his wife's head cut off. To this your wife might object...

'Again, as the play will probably run for a considerable time, your baby would grow. It might, therefore, be necessary to provide another baby. To this you and your wife might object – at short notice.' (vol. 1, pp. 116-7)

Other anecdotes found their way into contemporary newspapers around the world, such as this one reported in the *West Australian* (Perth):

Bram Stoker, who was with Henry Irving at the Lyceum for so many years, used to be pestered by people who wanted either to get at Irving himself or to get parts in a new play or, most frequently of all, to borrow money. One night, however, a man turned up who was a tragedian in what seemed to be deadly earnest. It was a dreadful night, rain falling, wind blowing, and the unlucky man was dressed in a rusty overcoat under which there did not seem to be any other garments. He asked to see Mr Stoker in an impressive voice and when they met, he explained that unless he could raise ten pounds there and then, he was going down to Waterloo Bridge to jump into the Thames. Bram Stoker took the man in at a glance and said: 'All right, my boy: I'm your man. I'm tired of life, too. Wait till I get my coat and I'll jump over with you!' (*West Australian*)

And there is humour where many would least expect to find it – in *Dracula*.

One should not be surprised to find comic elements in a novel such as *Dracula*. Humour delights in incongruity; and incongruity is embedded in all Gothic fiction. The sudden recognition of an incongruity can arouse either terror or laughter, or both. That Stoker is well aware of this paradox is made clear in Van Helsing's 'King Laugh' outburst in Chapter 13: the Professor explains his hysterical laughter in response to the horrible death of Lucy as 'his sense of humour asserting itself under very terrible conditions' (*Dracula*, p. 177). Two relevant points are raised here. First of all, laughter is often spontaneous rather than controlled. As we know all too well, we often laugh at the most inappropriate occasions, as if we are attempting to deflect or at least postpone a contemplation of reality. Second, and more importantly, laughter has a healthy function in that it provides emotional release from strain. Van Helsing is coping with the death of a beautiful young woman who was about to be married but has met a fate even worse than death – eternal damnation.

Comic traits also appear in the delineation of Quincey P. Morris, a character modelled to a great extent on William Cody ('Buffalo Bill') whom Stoker had met in London. Stoker plays with Morris's Texan idiom and slang. Also good for a chuckle are Van Helsing's broken English (Morris, he tells us, has a head 'in plane with the horizon') and Mina's jokes with the Professor about her shorthand notes. Bernard Davies points out in 'Inspirations, Imitations, and In-Jokes in *Dracula*' another form of Bram's comic sensibility that has risen to the surface in *Dracula*, his use of in-jokes intended solely for the person singled out. Perhaps the most prominent are directed at his close friend Angela, Baroness Burdett-Coutts: for example, he makes her, as chief shareholder in Coutts & Co., Count Dracula's banker.

The fun continued after *Dracula* was published. According to Bram's first biographer, Harry Ludlam, 'Noel [Bram's son] told me that in a flippant mood his father attributed the genesis of *Dracula* to a nightmare he had after a surfeit of dressed crab at supper one night. It was a private family joke' (p. 27), a joke that has been lost on many commentators who continue to insist that *Dracula* had its genesis in crab.

Similar anecdotes permeate the entire Journal, ranging from self-deprecation to witticism, from subtle to slapstick. There is also a goodly dose of darker humour, not surprising when one considers the fine line between laughter and tears. Nowhere is this more pronounced than in Irish humour, a topic to be explored more fully in Chapter 6.

## TRANSCRIPTIONS

### ⵝ 64 ⵝ

### *'A Counter-irritant'*

*An old woman shopping who doesn't buy.*

**1st of February, 1872**

*A waiter said a good thing to me last night. It was at a large party & he was one of the confectioner's men in the supper room. I was giving her supper to the young lady of the house & he was bringing in a fresh dish of cutlets into the room. So I said to him, 'Will you hand me that dish please', as there was a great crowd in the room & it was difficult to move about. He was a tall gaunt man with big cheek-bones and a large sense of his own importance. He evidently thought that the waiter was the man of the occasion. He looked at me seriously & firmly & then said wagging his head half-apologetically & with a deprecatory smile with some mirth & some sadness in it, 'Ah yes, sir. I'll help you if you like, but I can't give it to you. It wouldn't be fair'!!!*

30<sup>th</sup> of April, 1872

## ⤐ 66 ⇥

*Subject for Charade[39]: Syn-chronous Sin & Chronos.*

30<sup>th</sup> of April, 1872

## ⤐ 67 ⇥

*(ditto)*

*Islander I & slander.*

26<sup>th</sup> of January, 1873

## ⤐ 68 ⇥

*Carlile[40] saw a queer thing – a drunken woman eating a raw egg under the impression that it was an apple.*

28<sup>th</sup> of August, 1872

---

39  Charades is a game of guessing a word or phrase from the descriptive or dramatic representation of each syllable.

40  Hugh Carlile, a graduate of Trinity College and a contemporary of Bram's, would become a railway engineer in Russia.

*≈ 69 ≈*

*Three terms of humour are exaggeration, incongruity and contrast.*

27th **of October,** 1872 [Marg: Artemus Ward (C. F. Browne) thought they are essential][41]

*≈ 70 ≈*

*A clever man once copper bottomed the top of his house with sheet-lead.*

26th of January, 1873

*≈ 71 ≈*

*Dean [blank] of Manchester once in marrying 200 couples on Easter Monday made some mistake & joined the wrong people throughout the whole series. When remonstrated by some of the parties*

---

41     Artemus Ward was the nom-de-plume of American humourist Charles Farrar Browne, the favourite author of Abraham Lincoln and a source of inspiration for Mark Twain. This marginal note was added by Stoker.

*he said, 'Well never mind it now. You can sort each other when you get outside.'*

26<sup>th</sup> of January, 1873

⟿ 72 ⟿

*Q. What town in the County of Galway represents the 'whereas' of a typical Irishman addressing potential whisky?*
*A. 'Ah thin Rye!' (Athenry)*

⟿ 73 ⟿

*Q. Why would any man who had been osculated*[42] *by a feminine specimen of the Gallinaceous tribe*[43] *and observed by a male specimen of equine species be a fit leader of Saxon invaders?*
*A. Because he would be Henkissed & Horse saw (seen by a horse) (Hengest & Horsa)*[44]

27<sup>th</sup> of January, 1873

---

42  Embraced.

43  The Gallinacese are land birds that seek food on the surface. They include domestic fowl, pheasants, partridges and grouse.

44  Hengest and Horsa were two legendary Anglo-Saxon warriors.

## ⇢ 74 ⇠

*Q. Who was the fittest man that ever lived for building castles in the air?*
*A. Sir Christopher Wren![45]*

23rd of April, 1873

## ⇢ 75 ⇠

*Q. What scent is suggestive of anti–Elisha–ism?*
*A. Opoponax[46] (Elisha took a hatchet up out of the water,[47] which is the opposite to putting it up the spout.[48])*

12th of July, 1873

---

45    One of Britain's leading architects, he built fifty-one churches in the city of London after the Great Fire of 1666.

46    The resin of this herb can be burned as incense; it produces a balsam or lavender scent.

47    See II Kings 6:1–7.

48    'up the spout': British slang for pawned; in a desperate situation.

### ⇌ 76 ⇌

*Q. What fish reminds you of a 'the dansante'?*[49]
*A. A conger-eel (Congo reel).*[50]

18th of August, 1873

### ⇌ 77 ⇌

*Q. Why is death like a psalm?*
*A. Because kicking the bucket resembles a can tickle (canticle).*

12th of September, 1873

### ⇌ 78 ⇌

*Q. Why is Hamlet like a ballet?*
*A. Because there is a pa's soul (pas seul) in it.*

---

49  A 'the dansante' is 'a dancing tea'; i.e. rattling of cups and saucers.

50  'conger-eel': a scaleless predator; a strong and formidable antagonist.

### ⇒ 79 ⇐

*Description of a limp looking man: that he looked as if sent home from the wash without being starched.*

### ⇒ 80 ⇐

*T. P. A. Taggart[51] had a friend, a 'worm' farmer near Coleraine, who once gave a big dinner party. There were thirty guests and on being ushered into the dining room they found a bottle of champagne & a roast goose placed for each 'skull'.*

2nd of April, 1874

### ⇒ 81 ⇐

*Stewart K.'s father introduced Rᵗ <xxx> to ladies in his house as a clever young man who was only two months reading & got scholarship etc. & exam entry College prizes. On being asked not to do so again he introduced him as 'a young man of great*

---

51    T. P. A. Taggart is listed in 1858 as auditor for the Northern Bank in Coleraine.

talent & greater promise, but very bashful & as he
has an objection to his prizes being named I shall
say no more of them.'

⊷ 82 ⊶

There is one thing worse than pulling the devil by
the tail[52] – having no tail even of the devil to pull.

⊷ 83 ⊶

A man who had bought an insurance policy and
had a number of premiums complained to a friend,
'That man is immortal.'

⊷ 84 ⊶

Q. Why is the letter P like a Prince Consort?
A. Because it makes a Queen Regnant a Queen
pregnant.

---

52    'To pull the devil by the tail' is a colloquial phrase meaning 'to go to
      ruin headlong'.

## ⇢ 85 ⇠

*Q. What music is most suitable for a 'scratch'[53] party?*
*A. The Scotch fiddle.*

## ⇢ 86 ⇠

*A prisoner was described as being 'at the wrong side of the bar'.*

## ⇢ 87 ⇠

*To any one fond of a stretch how delicious must have been the first touch of pressure from the rack.*

## ⇢ 88 ⇠

*A Manchester merchant was bragging that his office afforded continuous work for 99 clerks. 'Why not have a hundred', said a friend 'if only to say that you had so many'. 'Well', he answered, 'You see so I have 100 clerks under pay: but then I only get work from 99. There is always one in the WC.'*

---

53    Made up of various sorts, likely just thrown together.

### ⊷ 89 ⊶

*Yankee name for a dog – a 'howling-piece'.*

### ⊷ 90 ⊶

*'A wholesale nose – nature started there a whole-sale nasal organ manufactory.'*

### ⊷ 91 ⊶

*Story of a man who wished for death and was thinking of suicide. Was cured by an attempt made to murder him. He fought hard & escaped. He did not choose that his life should be taken except with his own consent.*

21^st of August, 1875 [Marg: 'Try']

### ⊷ 92 ⊶

*Gastronomic triumphs 'Onion ices' & 'Oyster ices'.*

## ⇒ 93 ⇐

*He was a dirty ass. What do you think he did? He changed his name from Jones to Jones <xxx> & a few days afterwards whilst he was at his breakfast he went & turned round and died on the floor with an egg in his hand. C. L.*

## ⇒ 94 ⇐

*Q. Why was the father of Hannibal like a sucking pig?*
*A. Because he was a Hamilcar (Ham-milker)!*

## ⇒ 95 ⇐

*Cecil Roche[54] once in a speech of the Historical Society spoke of 'Prostitutes, thieves, policemen and the rest of the criminal classes'.*

---

54   This appears to be a reference to a judge in Listowel, reported to have been stern in his sentencing. Stoker creates such an individual in his story 'The Judge's House'.

## ⟶ 96 ⟵

*At servants' party Cullenswood*[55] *whilst a lady was singing 'The Bailiff's Daughter of Islington'*[56] *when she came to the part where 'She died sir long ago', one old man (Mr Mooney) remarked in an audible whisper, 'Oh dear oh dear, she knew how to get the dyin' grip on to him.'*

*The same man when he got home slightly the worse for his liquor gave his hat carefully to his wife and said to her, 'Take care now Molly how you use it an' just hang it nicely on a good strong peg.'*

## ⟶ 97 ⟵

*Asked a very old woman Granny before some girls: 'Now Granny, you are a woman of the world, answer me truly – do girls really object to being kissed as much as they pretend?'*

*She gave me a dig in the ribs and said, 'Ah go to God. <xxx xxx> half.'*

---

55   A suburban village on the outskirts of Dublin; now Ranelagh.

56   An old English Child ballad. The Child Ballads are a collection of 305 English and Scottish ballads, gathered for publication in the late nineteenth century by Francis James Child. 'The Bailiff's Daughter of Islington' dates back at least to the early seventeenth century.

## 98

*A man not rich wooed & won an heiress, his introduction to her being his bringing home the dead body of her brother. His friends said, 'It was the cold meat that did the business.'*

## 99

*A window cleaner fell from a second storey and got concussion of the brain. When he came out of hospital he said that he had had 'pincushion on the brain'.*

## 100

*A drunken man asked a traveller on the same road – 'How many clocks is it?' wanting to know the hour.*

## 101

*Irish expressions for drinking:*
*'Put it in your neck'*
*'To take the lining out of a tumbler of punch'*

### ⟿ 102 ⟼

*A misanthrope remarked, 'I like shooting: it is indeed a noble pastime. It is so inspiriting to hear the whish of the whips on the dogs and to see the blood of the birds flowing.'*

### ⟿ 103 ⟼

*George Sharpe[57] the artist was found by a friend who called, looking all about his studio for his palette which had stuck to the seat of his trousers – he had laid it on a chair & sat down on it.*

### ⟿ 104 ⟼

*A man noted for his jealousy once remarked among some friends on the subject of jealousy, 'That is a subject on which I have a fair right to give an opinion.'*

---

57   George Sharpe (1802–1877) was better known in Dublin as a teacher. As a painter, his methods were somewhat unorthodox. For example, he was accustomed to advise his pupils to always use a dirty paint brush in order to secure a low key of colour.

### ⊷ 105 ⊷

*1ˢᵗ Lady. 'I do not think it is much harm! Do you ever say d-a-m dam?'*

*2ⁿᵈ do[58] 'No, I never say it – but I sometimes think it very much.'*

*1ˢᵗ do 'And what do you do?'*

*2ⁿᵈ do 'I go up to my room and when I have the door locked and no one can see or hear, I stamp as hard as I can.'*

### ⊷ 106 ⊷

*C. Martelli saw a man in full Highland dress at a dinner of some Scotch Benevolent society in Dublin blowing his nose in his napkin.*

### ⊷ 107 ⊷

*Heard a man today speak of his wife as 'my mother-in-law's daughter'.*

**25ᵗʰ of February, 1876** [Marg: 'Old Hoggen'[59]]

---

58    Ditto.

59    A 'hoggen' has been defined as slang for an obese, over-madeup, under-dressed woman.

*A butcher in Howth*[60] *when remonstrated with for not taking off his hat to a wealthy customer said, 'There's only two places I take off my hat. The church and the police court. I take it off in the church because I think fairly that God is a bigger man than I am – and in the Court because if I didn't take it off it would be took off for me & I would be put in gaol.'*

⇥ 109 ⇤

*There was a widow's alms house in the south of England where by the will of a patron of the Charity a certain portion of meat was distributed amongst the inmates in equal proportions. One day there was a terrible uproar & the parson was sent for by the matron. The cause was this. It was the day for distributing the meat and it was accordingly effected at the usual time three of the inmates being absent. When these ladies came home & insisted*

---

60 Located on Howth Head, a peninsula just north of Dublin, Howth was a small harbour and fishing village. Still serving those purposes, it is now an affluent suburb of Dublin.

*that the meat should be brought back and put together like the pieces of a puzzle in order that they might satisfy themselves that they had got their fair amount and quality of the whole piece.*

22nd of July, 1876

⊷ **110** ⊶

*In Rathfriland[61] there was a woman who had dypsomania. Her husband locked her up but still she got liquor & after a time it was found that her servant used to give it to her by means of a pipe put through the keyhole.*

23rd of July, 1876

⊷ **111** ⊶

*Is not horseracing properly speaking a scientific (zoological) pursuit?*

---

61   Rathfriland is in Co. Down.

## ↠ 112 ↞

There are two kinds of love – amour propre and amour improper.

## ↠ 113 ↞

Miss Ellis told me of a farmer in Fermanagh whose wife was being confined for the first time. The doctor came out & told the father that he had a son & went in again. Presently he came out again and said he had a daughter also. The farmer looked grave. The doctor presently returned a third time and said, 'I must congratulate you again. Your wife has had another son.' The farmer took up his hat and said, 'Oh go on, go on. Then she may never stop', and went out of the house and was never heard of again.

## ↠ 114 ↞

Mild praise of good food: 'That is better than a tenpenny nail in your stomick.'

### ⇢ 115 ⇠

*In investigating title to a property – Carrowkeel Co. Sligo <xxx> found one man who flourished about 1690-1732 called 'Tumultuous McDonagh'.*

### ⇢ 116 ⇠

*The Rothschilds had just built (or had built) a new vessel for the mercury trade (to Calabor). The ship was on the stocks & was quite fitted & her crew all picked. The Captain, a Yankee, came to Lady R. & said, 'Wal ma'am, I calc'late we air in a little difficulty here about this ar ship.'*

*'What is it?' said Lady R.*

*'Wal, ye see ma'am, that the men won't go to sea in a ship that ain't christened & I have came to ask yer ladyship to be so kind as to christen her.'*

*'You forget', said the lady, 'that I cannot take part in any such ceremony. Do you not know that I am a Jewess?'*

*'Yes ma'am, I guess I du but still the men won't. Don't you be skeert just yet (seeing that she was getting angry). I calc'late there is a way out of the difficulty.'*

*'What is it?'*

*'Well ye see ma'am, we have considered the*

question on board & we have come to the conclu-
sion that ye can do as we want & yet do nothin' fur
to hurt yer feelin's either.'

'How is that?' said the lady. 'I fail to
comprehend.'

'Wal, ye see ma'am', said the captain with a
knowing smile & twirling his hat between his
fingers, 'Ye see ma'am that she air to be launched
with her stern foremost & if yer ladyship would
just take an axe and as she moves would jest
whittle a bit off the end of the bowsprit, I calc'late
it would correspond to the same ceremony.'

5th of February, 1877

⟜ **117** ⟞

In the firm of Gaussen & attorneys[62] the son of the
elder man who had just joined the business wrote
a business letter to the Earl of Charlemont beginning 'Our Lord'.

5th of February, 1877

---

62   This would be Gaussen, Chas. & Son, listed at 12 Gardiner Place,
     Dublin.

### ⇒ 118 ⇐

*During an election there was a demonstration against the unpopular candidate. The military were called out: the populace retreated behind a railing & pelted them with stones & when dislodged got into their homes & still pelted stones through the windows. The officer commanding got angry & called out, 'Cowards. You dirty cowards, why don't you come out & fight fair in the open like men.'*

*A man answered, 'Come out indeed! Not likely. For yous to get Crima-an medals & Victory crosses for stickin' yer bloody ba-nets up our a---h--e. Not likely!'*

### ⇒ 119 ⇐

*At an auction there was an old piano absolutely worthless. The owner said to auctioneer: 'Better give that to whoever will have it: it is not worth selling.'*

*'Ah sir, shure that's sure to sell. It'll do for some poor person who wants to use it for a sideboard – an' they'll git credit among their friends for keepin' a piany.'*

### ⊶ 120 ⊷

*There was a man at a small party of rustics who had a face exactly like that of a frog. His name was Wheatley but he was called Misther Croakley.*

### ⊶ 121 ⊷

*N. W. M. said that E. T. K. put his foot down easily to save his boots and walked without shaking so as not to rub or crease his clothes. 'If every man was as careful, tailors would be found dying by the hedgerows.'*

### ⊶ 122 ⊷

*Wm Carleton[63] the novelist was heard to say by me B. S., 'First you should lay a good solid foundation of healthy food – and then upon that you can pile up a noble & portly edifice of drink.'*

---

63 William Carleton (1794–1869) was a well-known Irish novelist with a propensity for heavy drinking. His most famous novel was *The Black Prophet: A Tale of Irish Famine* (1847).

## ⟠ 123 ⟠

*A drunken man was heard to say, 'Boys, I can't drink any more. Pour it over me.'*

## ⟠ 124 ⟠

*Heard Dr Nedley tell that he once heard Zozimus[64] say to boy who had stuck a pin in him a tergo, 'May the curse of an angry God light on the bloody lookin' scut that would stick a pin in a dark man's a\*\*e.'*

The oldest part of the Castle now standing is the Back Stairs. The entrance to this celebrated staircase is in the Castle Garden. After going up a few steps a passage is reached which leads by a kind of bridge, over the Lower Castle Yard, into the Castle. The steps of the stairs are iron; for so many people go up and down that if they were made of any softer substance they would have been worn away long ago.

The people who go up this stairs carry bags full of things and wear their hats very low over their faces. They generally have turnips, and gum-arabic, and steel pens, and penny packages of stationery in their bags. A man once told me that they sometimes bring the heads of people and sell them at the Castle; he also said that they of ten sell their country. Who could believe this?

I had heard so many stories about this Back Stairs that I made up my mind to go and see it for myself. Before setting out I resolved to humor the people in the Castle, whatever they might say to me. I got a bag, filled it with artichoke, and, having pulled my hat low over my eyes, went up.

When I got to the top I met a man who asked me "if I came about that affair." I said, "Yes," and he led me into a small room, where another man was eating the end of a large quill, and reading a large blue paper with writing on it, and having a large stamp in the corner. I sat down. "Did you come about that affair?" said he. "Yes," I answered. "Well,"

said he, "did you see him?" "I did," I answered. "What did he say?" he asked. "I don't know," said I, feeling just as if he would order me to be shot on the spot. "Good," he said; "I see you have been reading the Tichborne case and have learned caution from it. What have you in the bag?" "Artichokes." "How many?" "Twenty-five." "Were there really so many?" "Yes." "And 'choke him' were the words? Were they?" "Yes." "On the night of the 15th?" "Yes." "How much do you want for the artichokes?" "One hundred pounds." "Say two." "Two." "Gold or notes?" "Gold." "Very good! There you are," said he, handing me two small bags of sovereigns;" your information is most important. I shall forward it to the chief tonight. Good afternoon." And off I went with my two hundred sovereigns. -

The Castle is the best place in the world for selling artichokes and lilies. I would go with another bag of each now only the artichokes are out of season. Can you understand what information I gave? - I can't. I hope it wasn't against a Royal Residence or asphalting the streets of the city.

---

⊷⚞ **125** ⚟⊶

*I saw a scraggy old maid go through the bottom of a cane chair. Her feet stuck straight up over her head.*

⊷⚞ **126** ⚟⊶

*'Did you hear the latest move on the family chessboard?'*

⊷⚞ **127** ⚟⊶

*In the street:*
    *'It takes a gentleman to strike a blow like that.'*
    *'Yes – or a prizefighter.'*

⊷⚞ **128** ⚟⊶

*Names of persons (surnames)*
*Tumulty – Twabble*

⊷⚞ **129** ⚟⊶

*When a man or woman marries for money, the calculation as to the value of his or her portions is strange. Thus if a man marries a woman for*

*£10,000 her brain will roughly fetch &lt;xxx xxx&gt; if*
*he be a 12 st. man (50g) @ = 5.18.5 ¾ = £ 296 :3:11 ½*[65]
  *An eye would be worth*
  *A tooth*
  *The cap of the knee (patella)*
  *Nails each*
  *Eyebrows*

━━ 130 ━━

*In speaking of a pending divorce case a man said,*
*'Oh, it is merely a case of mistaken identity.' How?*
*'Well you see, the lady mistook the other man for*
*her husband.'*

━━ 131 ━━

*Dr Cameron said, 'I can always hear better with*
*an opera glass.'*

**24th of November, 1877**

---

65    Bram is obviously playing with a mathematical formula here. It leaves
    us puzzled.

### ⇢ 132 ⇠

*Dr Ledwich said one day to Dr O'Gdy*[66] *apropos of some experimental operation of the latter which had resulted fatally: 'I tell you what O'G. You are paving your way to hell with human corpses.'*

### ⇢ 133 ⇠

*An Irishwoman called to an Attorney (saving your presence) and asked him to get her a divorce from her husband.*

*'An' what is after bein' doin' to you now?'*
*'Shure sir, he hates me.'*
*'Oh that's nothin' at all at all.'*
*'Not if he hates me?'*
*'Nothin' at all. Is there anything else?'*
*'He is very cruel to the childhen.'*
*'Is that all?'*
*'All! Musha,*[67] *isn't that enough?'*

---

66   E. Ledwich and B. S. O'Grady are both listed in the *Medical Times and Gazette* (1877) as surgeons at Mercers Hospital in Dublin, and were professors of Anatomy and Surgery at Ledwich School of Anatomy, Medicine & Surgery on Peter St., Dublin.

67   'Musha' means 'indeed'.

'Begod my good woman, if that's all you have against your husband ye may as well go whistle jigs to a milestone as look for a divorce.'

'An' why not? He hates me, he is cruel to me childhen.'

'Look ye here, ma'am. The law doesn't mind that at all. In fact it thinks better of a man that beats his wife, for then there must be something against her. Is there anything else?'

'Well, sir', after a pause, 'I have reason to believe that he is unfaithful to me.'

'Ah now we're getting better. That's the best news yet. If he beats you and is unfaithful to you, we may get a divorce yet. Just wait till I shut the door & tell me all about it. Give me full details. And so he is unfaithful to you.'

'Yes sir, I have reason to believe that he is unfaithful to me.'

'Exactly what reason have you for your belief?'

'My belief, sur?'

'Yes, your belief.'

'Well sir' – another pause – 'I have reason to believe that he is not the father of my last child.'

⇥ 134 ⇤

*Heard two women talking in the street. One said to the other evidently talking of a third person, 'Well Mary, when you buy sin you ought to be very careful!'*

6th of September, 1878

⇥ 135 ⇤

*When I was at Lismore*[68] *(Dec. 1877) one Saturday night, there came into the coffee room of the hotel a very very stout redfaced woman, widow, her son a lad heavy & silent & two stout daughters. They drove in their new tax cart.*[69] *The lady called the waiter & asked at what price per head they could have tea & chops. Waiter answered 2/-. 'Mind', said the matron. 'We're to have as much as we can eat.' 'All right ma'am'. 'Mind', she reiterated, 'as much as ever we can eat, as much as we can put into us.'*

*'Oh ma'am, eat till yez burst.'*

---

68  Lismore is an island among the Inner Hebrides.

69  A light-springed cart upon which only a low rate of tax was charged.

*They did eat well. The lady herself ate twelve chops & the others did fairly also. Several times fresh tea had to be made & more dishes of chops & new bones brought. When all was done, the lady 'squeezed' the teapot & when the waiter was absent said, 'Yez must finish everything: it's sheer waste not to.'*

*When paying time came, the lady got her bill & went over it carefully & said to the waiter, 'Everything was very nice & there's sixpence for yourself.' The gratuity was a good one for a woman of her class to give & the waiter was pleased.*

*'Well didn't I tell yez I'd do it for yez – an' didn't I? Didn't I swell yez – eh?'*

⇀ 136 ↼

*Two drunken men were coming home by moonlight. As they got opposite to the lake, one said:*

*'Paddy, that's a fine moon.'*

*He looked critically at the splendid sheen of the moonlight on the water & said, 'Yes, begorra, it is a right good moon' & then added with drunken gravity, 'An' mind ye I'm hell-hard to please in moons.'*

In the north of Ireland, Co. Down, there was a christening. The parson who was long-winded & fond of hearing himself talk made a discourse before completing the ceremony. Said he:

'Well, my brethren, this is a very joyous occasion & a very solemn occasion too that brings us together here the day – an occasion, my brethren, calculated to make us thenk very seriously of thengs of the future. We come here for no other purpose than to christen this child an' if we just throw our thoughts a wee bit ahead, a thenk ye'll agree with me that the future of this child may be a very great future. Or perhaps it may not an' I can't tell you by myself whether it well or no. At the present time the child is certainly not much to look at – but no doubt as the time gets along that such a theng will most likely regulate itself. But the future of this child is the problem which only the fenger of history can solve. He may become even like I am myself – a menester of the gospel with great gifts of oratory & marvellous fluency of speech. He may in thes capacity go forth an' warfare against the heathen an' conquer the whole dollop – or in the more civilized & peaceful avocations of a menester of the gospel at home he may assert as we are doing now at the various forms & stages of propagating his kind of which the church takes very special notice & lest any of you should be thenkin' of thengs of which I don't touch I simply mean marryin' & christenin' & buryin' although I don't see how buryin' propagates much except it be they say that the dead make in process of discreet time an excellent garden mould for the fees is rather small. I know that they are there and although I learn that there are places where the generosity of the hearts of the people that dwell there oblige them to add something in the way of a wee present so as to bring the fees above the skenflent proportions fexed by the ecclesiastical conveniences. Well our young friend may be all this ay & much more too and may make a noise in the world as a preacher & what is more acquire great profit thereby.

'Or my brethren, this wee child may be a great soldier & may wen his way to glory & renown & fortune in the pleasant ways of an aide-de-camp or the baneful world of the commissariat – or perhaps he may die a glorious death fighting for the honour of his native land – perhaps he may win by his own valour a standard from the foe & thereby get promotion out of his turn without having to put money therefore into the hand of any man.

'Or perhaps he may become a great statesman who by the magnitude of his eloquence & by the vigour of his policy will be come in power in the land & whose tomb in Westminster Abbey may bear the words that he was born at Aughnocloy[70] & christened here, on the day on which we now are anno domini.

'Or perhaps he may be a great engineer – like Lesseps[71] or Hawkshaw[72] cutting canals from places that no one else wants to come from to fences that no man in his senses would willingly go to – & he may gain great repute & acquire much profit thereby.

'Or perhaps he may be a great surgeon or a great physician & may cut off enough limbs to pile up for himself an imperishable monument.

'Or yet he may be a sailor & carry the English flag over the seas after cevilizing the heathen by blowen' their bodies into fragments & their souls until Hell or else teaching them the noble lessons

---

70  A village in Co. Tyrone.

71  Ferdinand Marie, Vicomte de Lesseps (1805–1894) was the French developer of the Suez Canal, completed in 1869. He undertook a failed attempt to build a Panama Canal during the 1880s.

72  John Hawkshaw (1811–1891), an English civil engineer, was engaged in the construction of canals. In 1871 he became engineer for the Channel Tunnel Company. His son attended TCD during the 1860s.

of romance which the heathen are only too <xxx> to learn by drinking plenty of the best they can get & then slaying one another just to promote merit.

'Or my brethren, there are many other ways in which this child may shine & leave a great & shining example to us all but the day is drawin' en & its about time we were all getting' something to eat, so I will just call on the father to name the child.'

The father was a tall man & he was a wee bit deaf & he ups & he says, 'What?'

'I call on ye', says the menester, 'to name this child'.

The father ups again & he says, 'Mary Anne'.

For it wur a gerl.

## ⇢ 138 ⇠

### 'Epigram'

by Dr Tisdall of Dublin, Chancellor of Christ Church, on hearing Pusey[73] with a bad cold & cough preaching at St Mary's Church, Oxford.

---

73   Edward Bouverie Pusey was a high-church Anglican (in)famous for preaching obsolete doctrines.

*How disappointing the effect*
*On Pusey's congregation*
*For the oration they expect*
*They get expectoration.*

⇥ 139 ⇤

*'Augury'*

He: *'How did you try the augury of the ships?'*

She: *'I said if there be four I shall have hope.'*

He: *'Did you do it more than once?'*

She: *'Often & often!'*

He: *'Were there ever four?'*

She: *'Often & often!'*

He: *'And when there were not?'*

She: *'Then I tried again & again till there were!'*

### ⟢ 140 ⟡

*At an Irish funeral the officiating clergyman in a pause of the service suddenly burst out laughing after the sexton had whispered something to him. He explained it afterwards when reproached for the scandal:*

*'I really could not help it. Rafferty came & whispered to me in a most solemn manner, "If ye plaze sorr, the brother of the corpse wants to have a word wid ye"!'*

### ⟢ 141 ⟡

*W. M. Woodroffe[74] told me today the following:*

*An Irishman (labourer) applied for a job. The employer, not accepting him as skilled in any way, asked: 'What can you do? What kind of work?'*

*'I can do any kind of work.'*

*'Can you make a venetian blind?'*

*'I can aisy.'*

---

74　William Morton Woodroffe was the father of William Litton Woodroffe, one of Bram's fellow students at TCD.

*The employer, doubtful. 'Now how would you do it?'*

*Labourer – confident, 'Begor I'd give him a poke in th'oi!'*

21st of March, 1871[75]

---

75    This entry was obviously written earlier and possibly copied into the Journal years after original composition.

## Child's Love

"Oos very ugly" said the child: and this set me
thinking.

It is not at any time very pleasant to be
called ugly. particularly when you know that
accusation is true. It is particularly unpleasant
be told an unpleasant truth by a child. There is
something so artless, and naive in the manner
which it is done. something so hopeless in the
itself. From a grown person a truth need not be a full
truth. malice or good will. ignorance or tact can
change or modify it. but from a child's lips a truth
a truth. The mind which frames the remark & the
lips which utter it are all too guileless and
innocent to think of effects produced or
means to be used in producing them. All is
perfect, naked, undisguised truth. the child
seems almost unconscious of what it says.
Its words are the spontaneous outpourings
its mind. it knows nothing of artifice.
concealment. it speaks as it feels & it
speaks because it thinks and it thinks
because it feels. Its half awakened
intelligence can grasp easily and truthfully

# FOUR

# ⇒ PERSONAL AND ⇐ DOMESTIC

On first sight, the Journal contains very few truly personal comments such as one might find in a diary. Yet a careful reading of the entries in light of what we do know about Bram's life and relationships reveals much more than initially meets the eye. Several of the early notes, for example, touch on the theme of loneliness, providing us with rare glimpses into his inner self. Much of this sense of loneliness derives from his own childhood.

Bram (Abraham) Stoker was born in Clontarf (now part of the city of Dublin) on 8 November 1847 and spent his earliest years at 15 Marino Crescent. The third of seven children born to Abraham and Charlotte

Stoker, Bram stood out from his siblings in that he was a sickly child. As he recalled years later in 1906, 'In my babyhood I used, I understand, to be often at the point of death. Certainly till I was about seven years old I never knew what it was to stand upright' (*Personal Reminiscences*, vol. 1, p. 31). Deleted from the unpublished manuscript we find a few additional observations by Bram about his first seven years:

> When the nursery bell rang at night my mother would run to the room expecting to find me dying. All my early recollection is of being carried in people's arms and of being laid down somewhere or other on a bed or a sofa if within the house, on a rug or amid cushions on the grass if the weather was fine. (qtd in Belford, p. 14)

In spite of the preponderance of medical doctors in the Stoker family, no explanation for this mysterious illness has ever been provided. Not surprisingly, there are theories: rheumatic fever, an unidentified illness lurking in the shadows of the Irish famines and plagues, or a misdiagnosis of a heart condition that required bed rest. Maybe it was psychosomatic; maybe it was a romantic fantasy conjured up later, fed by Byronic poetry. Family members believe that Bram was the victim of a weak immune system that left him vulnerable to numerous childhood ailments including allergies and asthma, a condition prevalent in several Stokers to this very day. A respiratory problem would have been exacerbated by living in moist conditions by the sea at Clontarf. Constant dampness and the ensuing mould and mildew may have precipitated the family's move further inland to Killester and Artane when Bram was just a few years old. Whatever the nature of his illness, by the time Bram reached his eighth year, his condition began to improve. Since his recovery was complete, with no long-term residual damage, it is doubtful that he suffered from a serious disease.

The theory of a weak immune system receives a boost from the fact that Bram's great-grandsons remember that their grandfather Noel Stoker was not a robust man, and had not been a robust boy. In the stories of his childhood, there was nothing to suggest that Noel Stoker was athletic; rather he was sensitive and shy, and seemed by their description to border on frailty. Was there something of a common condition in their early years between father and son? One could further speculate that Bram, growing up in the midst of a family of healthy and outgoing personalities, made a more conscious decision to get well than did his son, an only child, without a house full of active playmates. 'This early weakness', Bram would recall, 'passed away in time and I grew into a strong boy and in time enlarged to the biggest member of my family. When I was in my twentieth year I was Athletic Champion of Dublin University' (*Personal Reminiscences*, vol. 1, pp. 31-32).

FEVER HOSPITAL AND HOUSE OF RECOVERY, IN DUBLIN.

ILLUSTRATED BY CASES.

BY WILLIAM STOKER, M. D.

*April the 8th.*—Very little blood taken by the lancet, but a very copious discharge from the leeches; began to sleep soon after the bleeding ceased. The purgative medicines caused seven copious stools; the eyes are less fixed; the pupils more contractile; can swallow a little better, but with a rattling sound; muscles of the jaws and back less rigid; less agitation of the head; pulse more distinct; skin softer, and petechiæ rather fainter; passed some urine unconsciously, as she did the stools also; used all her medicines as prescribed;

Although no records have been found to substantiate Bram's illness or treatment, family lore has long contended that an uncle, Dr Edward Stoker, cared for him, and that he was bloodlet, a common medical procedure of the day used to drain out some of the 'bad blood' thought to be causing the unknown malady. Bloodletting was a favoured treatment for inflammation, and found to be helpful during early stages of bronchitis, croup, pneumonia and meningitis. Dr Stoker's father, Dr William Stoker, was a well-known proponent of the practice, both by lancet and leech.

In retrospect, Bram would write that those years had given 'opportunity for many thoughts which were fruitful according to their kind in later years' (*Personal Reminiscences*, vol. I, p. 31). While his siblings ran about freely, he lay in bed, captive and vulnerable. His mother filled many of his hours with stories and legends from her native Sligo, including supernatural tales and narratives of disease and death, surely a major factor in the nurturing of a Gothic sensibility that would make its presence felt in much of his later writing, including *Dracula*.

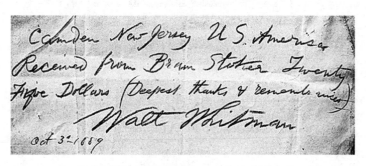

*An IOU from Walt Whitman to Bram Stoker*

But what of more pronounced effects on his developing personality? In a letter to Walt Whitman written in 1872, Bram indicated that he was 'naturally secretive to the world'. Such reticence was due in part to those many long hours spent living within himself and internalising his thoughts. His decision to keep a journal was as much a desire to open up (at least to himself) as it was a gathering of potential material for some future writing endeavours.

In several of his scribblings, he muses on children, loneliness and abandonment. His sensitivity to children reflects a deep-rooted need to connect, to compensate for the isolation that blanketed him for the first seven years of his life. 'I felt as tho' I were my own child,' he wrote plaintively. 'I feel an infinite pity for myself. Poor, poor little lonely child' (153). Another entry is equally poignant: 'Will men ever believe that a strong man can have a woman's heart & the wishes of a lonely child? … If ever the time do come I would like to steal back a moment in the twilight and whisper a prayer in some child's ear that hearing my whisper it might feel happy & no longer lonely' (142). The loneliness and desire to reach out is also evident in entry 143.

One also detects a sense of self-consciousness and self-effacement, possibly the consequence of vulnerability and helplessness. This is most conspicuous in the detailed account he writes about a child that he and his companions met on the beach at Greystones.

'Oos very ugly', said the child, and this set me a-thinking. It is not at any time very pleasant to be called ugly, particularly when you know that the accusation is true. It is particularly unpleasant to be told an unpleasant truth by a child. There is something so artless and naive in the manner in which it is done: something so hopeless in the thing itself. From a grown person a truth need not be a full truth. Malice or good will, ignorance or tact may change or modify it. But from a child's lips a truth is a truth. (143)

This self-consciousness about his appearance crops up just a few months later (in 1872) in a most unusual place – the letter to Walt Whitman.

This letter, written primarily in defence of Whitman's poetry, includes a description of his own physical appearance in remarkable detail:

I am six feet two inches high and twelve stone weight naked and used to be forty-one or forty-two inches round the chest. I am ugly but strong and determined and have a large bump over my eyebrows. I have a heavy jaw and a big mouth and thick lips – sensitive nostrils – a snub nose and straight hair… I am equal in temper and cool in disposition and have a large amount of self-control and am naturally secretive to the world. I take

> a delight in letting people I don't like – people of mean
> or cruel or sneaking or cowardly disposition – see the
> worst side of me. (qtd in Belford, pp. 42–3)

That Bram thought himself unattractive, when all surviving photos show an attractive, handsome man is quite revealing. The references to his 'ugly' looks and the bump on his forehead reinforce the self-conscious-ness evident in the entry about the child on the beach.

Children are prominent in much of his writing. His first book of fiction, *Under the Sunset* (1881), was a collection of stories for children, dedicated to his own son, Noel. The moral emphasis on goodness, a dominant theme in the incident with the child on the Greystones beach, reverberates in many of them, most notably 'Lies and Lilies' and 'The Wondrous Child'. Two other stories deal with themes that may well have had their genesis in his early bed-ridden years: fear and loss, pain and grief, madness and death. In 'The Shadow Builder', an odd tale that combines elements of Plato's myth of the cave and Robinson Crusoe, a mother saves her son from the jaws of death, leading the narrator to conclude that 'the Mother's arms are stronger than the grasp of death'. 'The Invisible Giant' with his 'grim spectral hands' represents the threat and fear of plague. Children reappear in some of his later work, most notably in *Dracula*, as vulnerable and helpless victims of the vampiric Lucy on Hampstead Heath.

A few of the entries hint at domestic life in the Stoker family: the New Years' Eve revelries of the cook (144); a comment made by the family nurse (145); and a reference to Bram's youngest brother George (159). There is a curious allusion to his mother Charlotte (158); curious, because he does not identify her as the source of this anecdote. However, Harry Ludlam records this story from Bram's son Noel about her: 'We laughed at Charlotte's foibles. Such as her advice to people when taking a horse-cab. She maintained that as Dublin cabmen were not famed for their civility it was best to stop and alight at a chapel or a policeman, whichever was nearest to the house' (*My Quest for Bram Stoker*, p. 31).

'When God made that woman He broke the mould,' Bram wrote in his Journal (150). A few of his entries (152, 155, 160, 162) hint at an interest in women, though none of them are specific. Then we have the mystery of Bessie L'Estrange, the woman whose name shapes Bram's earliest known poem 'Acrostic' (see p. 48–9). Available evidence about this relationship is far from conclusive. There was a Bessie L'Estrange – born 1812, married 1835, died 1890 – an unlikely candidate given her age. But she was married to William Ledwich, possibly the same Ledwich Bram mentions in another entry (see p. 107). Maybe the 'love poem' was written with tongue planted firmly in cheek! Another Bessie L'Estrange (née Matthews) may have had a granddaughter (closer in age to Bram) who bore her name. But none of this can be confirmed. This remains an unsolved mystery.

We know that Bram cultivated close friendships with several prominent women of his day. He maintained a relationship with actress Genevieve Ward, was close to artist Pamela Colman Smith and was adored by Ellen Terry. Terry had this to say of him in her own memoir, *The Story of My Life*:

> Bram Stoker, whose recently published 'Reminiscences of Irving' have told, as well as it ever can be told, the history of the Lyceum Theatre under Irving's direction, was as good a servant in the front of the theatre as Loveday was on the stage. Like a true Irishman, he has given me some lovely blarney in his book. He has also told all the stories that I might have told, and described every one connected with the Lyceum except himself. I can fill that deficiency to a certain extent by saying that he is one of the most kind and tender-hearted of men. He filled a difficult position with great tact, and was

not so universally abused as most business managers, because he was always straight with the company, and never took a mean advantage of them.

Bram numbered among his closest friends Angela, Baroness Burdett-Coutts. She became the richest woman in England when still quite young, and was the friend of many of the famous men of her time: the Emperor Napoleon III, the Duke of Wellington, Charles Dickens and Sir Henry Irving. But she seems to have found Bram Stoker, with his boyish sense of fun, more relaxing company than Irving.

Not all of the comments about women scattered throughout the Journal are complimentary. At times we sense a typically Victorian male, responding to women in a standard Victorian manner: a comment about woman as Eve (160), an assertion of the superiority of man over woman (161) and a satirical swipe at woman's vanity (162). We see the same ambivalence about women that informs much of the novel *Dracula*. Nowhere does Stoker focus on this ambiguity more forcefully than in his characterization of Mina. As Clive Leatherdale succinctly notes in *Dracula: The Novel & the Legend*, 'She adopts certain modern trappings associated with the New Woman, while remaining at heart a devoutly traditional female' (p. 148). Unlike Lucy who succumbs readily to the Count's advances, Mina not only resists but plays a key role in the pursuit and destruction of the vampire.

Bram began courting his future wife, Florence Balcombe, reputedly (according to George du Maurier) one of the three most beautiful women in Dublin, as her interest in Oscar Wilde waned. Florence had met Oscar in 1876, a summer he spent swimming, riding and playing lawn tennis in Dublin. He wrote to a friend that Florence was 'exquisitely pretty', with the 'most perfectly beautiful face I ever saw and not a sixpence of money' (qtd in Belford, p. 85). She was seventeen, and Oscar must have seemed worldly and charming. Although he was attending Oxford, they began a relationship that lasted – at least in Oscar's mind – until just a few months before her marriage to Bram in December 1878.

Letters illustrate Oscar's lack of attention to Florence, his wanderlust, as well as his general disregard for convention, any of which could have caused her to set her sights elsewhere. Oscar travelled abroad with friends when he should have been at Oxford, and after short visits to Dublin, his vacations were spent hunting and fishing. In March of 1878, he was in Dublin for four days, but did not see Florence, which he later tried to excuse in a letter. That summer, instead of spending time in Dublin, he took a holiday in the western mountains of Ireland. If he had been more attentive, Oscar may not have learned of her engagement to Bram from someone else, a fact he lamented in a letter to request she return a small gold cross he had given her (see Miller, *Bram Stoker's Dracula: A Documentary Journey*, pp. 17–19).

Although friends, Bram and Oscar were not close and were cut from different cloth. Bram's solid character and traditional values would have been in stark contrast to Oscar, who was working to perfect his image as a gadabout and a dandy. Bram was a gentleman with a permanent job and a steady income, and his association with the theatre and his developing relationship with Henry Irving had to be alluring to a young, aspiring actress. Finally, Florence knew Oscar well enough to realise a life with him would be filled with frustration and uncertainty.

Within a few months, Florence Balcombe and Bram Stoker were wed. She was nineteen, he was thirty-one. The marriage took place at St Ann's Church, Dawson St., on Wednesday 4 December 1878. Witness was Bram's friend from his years at Trinity College, Thomas W. Martelli. Only five days after the wedding, with no time for a honeymoon, Bram and Florence moved to London. Noel, their sole child, was born just over a year later in December 1879. The family lived first in Bloomsbury, then moved the following year to 27 Cheyne Walk in Chelsea. The 1881 census lists as other occupants of the house a nurse, a cook and a housemaid.

Much speculation exists to this day about the marital relationship between Bram and Florence. Unfortunately, the Journal sheds no new light on this matter. There is, however, one entry that captures at least one moment of domestic tenderness involving the two of them and their baby (165).

## TRANSCRIPTIONS

### ⋯⇒ 142 ⇐⋯

*'Sympathy'*

*How is this? I feel so lonely. Men and women pass me every moment and as I glance into their faces I seem to see inmost yearning like my own. Some of the faces are marked by care & pain & the shadow of some great sorrow is over many such faces. I long to draw forwards and let them rest against my bosom where they may at least find a calm for a moment in the thought that there is a heart that feels with them. Some return my look & seem to long to spring to me & rest but the gleam of hope that rises in my soul dies away: the shadow of the world with its palaces, its churches & its prisons, comes down upon the faces and the yearning look turns to distrust and the sympathy turns to pride – and then a dull dead feeling comes over me, as if a friend whom I loved and trusted had turned and struck me, and the hope dies away and the shadows that I see before me grow stronger than the lights and I feel as if a great wrong had been done to make one heart hard & distrustful & to make another ache. Then for a time I go on & the old life springs up again fresh and green & my heart is larger and fuller than ever and in its thought of the former rebuffs grows humbler & meeker & is content to love without expecting love in return.*

*And yet with all this feeling, when I try to speak the same mistrust comes over myself & the repentance for it makes me long, oh so much, for some shoulder on which to lay my own head and weep – and tell all my little pains and griefs. Eagerly I peer into all faces which I see but the look of pity which I feel for others comes not to me. If it did, oh how my heart would bound with joy – it may come yet.*

*Oh if men but knew each others' hearts what misery would be saved for many. If each man would think that every brother & sister under Heaven has a heart that beats like his own with the same joys and sorrows. The dream makes me sad.*

*Let me feel in my own heart a deep sympathy for all – and most of all for those who have no sympathy, for their lot must be hard indeed. Will men ever believe that a strong man can have a woman's heart & the wishes of a lonely child? It may be so: but if ever the time do come I would like to steal back a moment in the twilight and whisper a prayer in some child's ear that hearing my whisper it might feel happy & no longer lonely.*

Greystones, 5th of August, 1871

⟿ 143 ⟾

### 'Child's Love'

'Oos very ugly', said the child, and this set me a-thinking.

*It is not at any time very pleasant to be called ugly, particularly when you know that the accusation is true. It is particularly unpleasant to be told an unpleasant truth by a child. There is something so artless and naive in the manner in which it is done: something so hopeless in the thing itself. From a grown person a truth need not be a full truth. Malice or good will, ignorance or tact may change or modify it. But from a child's lips a truth is a truth. The mind which frames the remark & the lips which utter it are all too guileless and too innocent to think of effects produced or the means to be used in producing them. All is perfect, naked, undisguised truth. The child seems almost unconscious of what it says. Its words are the spontaneous outpourings of its mind. It knows nothing of artifice or concealment. It speaks as it feels and it speaks because it thinks and it thinks because it feels. Its half awakened intelligence can grasp easily and truthfully all external manifestations and appearances. It is truthful because of its intelligence and it speaks because it is truthful.*

*And yet the child does not judge by external appearances. It has some delicate sympathy – call it not instinct – which tells it of things within & beyond external form. The child whose remark set me thinking liked me the first time it saw me. She[76] looked on at me for a minute or so & then*

---

76    Here and at the beginning of the next sentence, Stoker seems to have changed 'He' to 'She'.

crept up to my side & caught hold of my hand. She is an ugly child, more than usually ugly with a face more like an old woman's than a child's. Broad and discoloured with jagged uneven teeth and with an immense ugly mouth, close broad deep upper lip projects and curls with every varying expression that can flit over a child's face, and is covered already with a sort of down. Her cheeks broaden out round the eyes as she laughs, and her eyes are rebellious looking and mischievous.

When first I felt the touch of the little thing's hand her trustfulness & affection caught my attention & I stooped and looked at her. She put up her face for a kiss. Since then she clings to me on every occasion and does not seem happy when she is near me unless she is sitting on my knee or holding my hand. At first she used to whisper child's commonplaces & turn away her head bashful & laughing. Today she put up her face & after looking at me for a long time whispered in my ear the words which set me thinking: 'Oos very ugly'. And having said so she clung close to me.

Now what I want to know is: by what feelings was that child stirred? It could not be pity for that would imply an understanding of the value of beauty in giving power to the owner. It could not be *that she felt sympathy for my ugliness on account of her own, for that would imply that she knew it – a thing quite impossible for a child seven years old; and yet she clung closer to me when she said it.*

*It must have been that she had established a confidence between us, that she had given voice to a connection that had grown within her mind. She had no fear for my offended vanity if such should be, but she evidently trusted me – and that feeling so spontaneously shown far, far more than counteracted any pain that the consciousness of a physical deformity could give me under any circumstances whatever.*

*Some hours after, five or six of us walked along the shore – the child among the number. She was troublesome & wanted to hold my hand and run about but I told her I could not give her my hand as she would want to play. Bye & bye she rolled in the sand & got up laughing. Her sister told her she must not do it & accordingly she did it again several times. Her sister told me that she was exceedingly obstinate & self-willed. I told her that she must be good whereupon she laughed & flung herself down again. I told her again quietly and firmly that she must be good & do as she was told. Still no answer so I turned and walked on. Bye & bye up came the little truant & laughing caught my hand. I took it away quietly telling her that she must not touch me till she was good. She laughed gleefully.*

*Presently we sat down & she went to sit on my legs as I lay on the beach. I put her gently off, telling her that she must not touch me till she was good. Presently she got up & walked down to the sea & came back & timidly came behind me & tried to kiss me. 'No', said I, 'only good children must touch me or come near me.' She sat silent beside her sister & looked at me. I asked her would she be good, she laughed and said 'no'. For a few minutes we elders talked & the child looked at me wistfully, making little 'moves' as if to ask to be allowed to kiss me. I felt pained that I had to look sternly at her but I should be firm.*

*I was digging holes with my hand in the shingle & she joined in timidly, little by little, as if trying how far I would make hence. I stopped, looked at her firmly & said that she must not play with me till she was good. She looked at me firmly & intently & wistfully and then turned away. I felt really pained but I should teach her a lesson. Bye & bye she burst out crying. I said, 'Be you good now. Will you do always what you are told?'*

'*Ya*'.

'*What is it you say? Speak out plainly. I am very serious.*'

'*Yes*', *and her lip quivered.*

'*Shake hands*', *I said and held out my brawny palm, she put her little mite of a hand into it & seeing that she could not squeeze it she pressed with her other hand my fingers down on hers. She rose and sat down on my legs & then stooping threw some sand into my sand pits & then coming up close to me said in a whisper,* '*May I kiss oo*', *and seeing an answer in my eyes, kissed my cheek & then sat down on the sand & nestled close to me. I thought that I had found the cause of her liking for me – she trusted me & respected me for she saw that I was stronger in will than she was. Though I believe in my inmost heart I am not vain of personal appearance & tho' I can say honestly that her expression 'oo is very ugly' did not harm or wound me but merely set me thinking, still I felt a glad feeling when she showed her trust & faith in me. I thought then, I think now, that it was the artist that spoke & not the child.*

**Greystones, 6ᵗʰ of August, 1871, 11½ PM**[77]

---

[77]  Obviously written at night at local lodging.

⊷ 144 ⊷

*'Clock right with Barracks'*[78]

*I said to the new cook (a very pretty looking girl of about 24) who was coming down the stairs, 'Kate, is this clock right?'*

*'Oh yes sir, quite.'*

*'Is it right by the railway station [which is opposite the house]?'*

*'Well sir, I don't know whether it's right by the Railway but it certainly is by the Barracks.'*

*(I went out quickly, thinking.)*

1st of January, 1872[79]

---

78    At this time Bram was still living with his parents on Harcourt St., in
      a house directly across from the railway station. The nearest barracks
      would have been Portobello, about a fifteen-minute walk to the
      southwest.

79    New Year's Day.

⇥⇥ 145 ⇥⇥

*It was a common saying of our old nurse Ellen Crone,*[80] *'You would do little for God's sake if the devil was dead.'*

30th of April, 1872

⇥⇥ 146 ⇥⇥

*As the sleep that comes over us against our will unconquerable yet delicious to be overcome by is love to a woman.*

3rd of January, 1874

⇥⇥ 147 ⇥⇥

*A woman shaking her fist at a man is as good as her marriage lines.*[81]

---

80   Ellen Crone worked with the Stoker family from the 1840s and was employed there when she died in 1869. Bram's oldest brother, William Thornley, kept a photograph of her in an envelope along with a lock of her hair throughout his life. He also kept a photo of her gravestone at Rathfarnham Graveyard, Dublin.

81   In palmistry, 'marriage lines' are the horizontal lines on the Mount of

⊷ 148 ⊷

*At Clarisford[82] there is a Birds' Burial Ground made by the children. All the little graves are regularly made & planted with small flowers: and there are headstones made of slate & engraved with the dates of birth & death & the names and verses of poetry.*

⊷ 149 ⊷

*'A mother's arms are always strong enough to carry her child.'*

⊷ 150 ⊷

*'When God made that woman He broke the mould.'*[83]

---

Mercury below the little finger.

82    There is a slate quarry near Clarisford House, Killaloe, the residence of George F. Fitzgerald (TCD physics professor) and his brother William, who would illustrate Stoker's *Under the Sunset*. Stoker incorporated this description of the Burial Ground into 'How 7 Went Mad', one of the stories in that collection.

83    We do not know whether the reference is to any specific woman, or even whether this quotation was his own.

⟿ 151 ⟸

*Love can only be made in perfection beside the sea.*

⟿ 152 ⟸

*No matter whom a woman may have loved, when she marries her love goes to her husband. He is the Aaron's rod*[84] *that swallows up all the others.*

⟿ 153 ⟸

*I felt as tho' I were my own child – I feel an infinite pity for myself – Poor, poor little lonely child.*

⟿ 154 ⟸

*A mother was trying to teach her little girl about the Trinity & the child was puzzled about the Three in One. At last she said, 'Oh mother I know now. It is just like when there are three candles in the room but only one light.'*

---

84  Biblical reference to the brother of Moses. Aaron's rod miraculously turned into a snake and consumed the rods/snakes of the Pharaoh (Exodus 7:8–13).

### ⇥ 155 ⇤

*'If a woman really loved a man she would marry him even if she had to live in a cab.'*

### ⇥ 156 ⇤

*'Dream of old woman & old soldier'*

*I dreamed 29/2/76 that some military spectacle was going on down in the Nth Bull at Dollymount.*[85] *I was walking through the fallen leaves & many other persons on foot in carriages & on horseback were going on the same road. I saw before me an old woman whose face I thought I knew. She was bent & wrinkled, shabbily dressed in black, but old clothes cut into newest fashion. Her yellow wrinkled face was filthy dirty with the yellow-ish discolouration of those who never wash – & it was painted and powdered. She walked along with a juvenile jaunty strut – sadly marred by her infirm old knees & rheumatic feet. She was flirt-ing violently with an old man in dress of Capn*

---

85   In Clontarf, on North Bull Island, the beach is called Dollymount Strand. It was a popular gathering place.

*of grenadier guards. He too was a spectacle. His uniform was literally in rags. His shape was as if mangy. His tunic all discoloured and worn, his black trousers with patches themselves worn away. His drill boots were burst all out at the sides so that the ragged edges projected an inch beyond the foot. His gloves were worn to rags about the fingers. He too walked as jauntily as age, gout & rheumatism would let him, with his sword tucked under his arm & bending down to whisper to his companion. The old lady introduced me as I came up. 'This is dear Capt Blake,[86] master my dear of the guards, an old flame of mine.' I had a pocket handkerchief in my hand & the old clean shaven hollow eyed dear man said entreatingly, 'May I use it too' & seized it. I thought the best way out of it was hastiness so said, pressing the handkerchief into his hand, 'You shall have a present of it, my dear boy.' Not another word & I woke.*

29<sup>th</sup> of March, 1876 morn.

---

86     Charlotte Stoker's mother (Bram's grandmother) Matilda was a Blake who married Thomas Thornley.

## ⇒ 157 ⇐

*Saw a kitten[87] run over the keys of the piano tonight. At first sound astonished – then frightened & running for her life, jumping to the floor & disappearing through the door like a streak of lightning.*

## ⇒ 158 ⇐

*A certain old lady[88] who has an idea that all cabmen are villains sometimes tells her driver to stop close to the convent. She is a Protestant & believes the worst of the whole Catholic world but she seeks the sanctuary of the convent. Her more common direction is, 'Please drive slowly & carefully to so & so – when you get near the place stop close to a policeman.'*

---

87    According to his son Noel (as told to Ludlam) Stoker was fond of cats; his household always had one.

88    Although Stoker does not identify the lady, family lore has it that this was one of Charlotte's foibles. The incident is mentioned in Ludlam (p. 77) but without the reference to Catholicism.

## ⇢▰ 159 ▰⇠

*Speaking of George Stoker, Chef de l'Ambulance du Croissant Rouge in Turkey, Dr Malone said, 'Mrs Stoker[89] seemed to be in some fear for him. She seemed to think that just then the Russians might be taking him with onions.'*

## ⇢▰ 160 ▰⇠

### 'The Lost'

*'Man lures us down through the portals of Heaven. But the hand of a woman would thrust us to Hell.'*

## ⇢▰ 161 ▰⇠

### 'Tact & Truth'

*'A woman's tact goes down before a man's truth like grass before the mower, like wax before the flame.'*

---

89    This must be a reference to Charlotte (George's mother) as he would not marry Agnes McGillycuddy until 1884.

## ⟶ 162 ⟵

*A true woman has two good friends – her Bible and her looking-glass.*

## ⟶ 163 ⟵

*Love in its youth has the edge of a razor – in its age that of a dinner knife. It is well to keep the primal edge as long as possible. Yet how many by little notches reduce it systematically as soon as possible all unintending – a breath tarnishes the polish of the razor – but this fades in the light of a smile etc.*

**8th of September, 1878**[90]

## ⟶ 164 ⟵

*A woman's judgement of a man*
*'Now he is a man one could marry.'*

**F. S.**[91]

---

90   When he wrote this entry, Bram was courting Florence Balcombe. They would marry three months later.

91   Florence Stoker.

*Florence Stoker and baby Noel*

⊸ **165** ⊷

*The Baby was going into town with F. & the nurse. There was a levee*[92] *on so I said to F.*

*'You ought to take the Babe & show him to the Queen.'*

*She answers, 'Indeed I shall do no such thing.'*

*'Why?' I asked.*

*'Because she would want to put him in her crown.'*

[Marg: FS 1880][93]

---

92   A 'levee' is a reception or social gathering. The term was originally used in Great Britain to refer specifically to a public court assembly held in the early afternoon to which only males were invited.

93   Noel was born in London in December 1879.

Horan and three other men once had lodgings in Gard[en]
St Lower. They had taken them by the quarter; but after a f[ew]
weeks found that their landlady plundered them fearfully. [once]
this they opened a bottle of sherry & placed it in a cupboa[rd]
& no one touched it, still it got less & less till it was [gone]
Whole joints disappeared &c. When they said they would
stay any longer, and got other lodgings. The landlady
then she would not let them go & would if necessary [forgive]
[for] rent.

They said very well & stayed.

They always breakfasted & dined out so that there [was]
no plunder. They came home very late & one by [one]
& each one knocked up the house. They gave t[he]
parties lasting till 4 or 5 o'clock, with dances. [They]
gave musical parties with horns & a drum. &
friends to call always for some of them when [coming]
home from parties at the small hours.

At the end of the second week the landl[ady]
implored them to go & offered to let them off [the]
rent due.

FIVE

# ⊷ FRIENDS AND ⊷
# ACQUAINTANCES

'Never in any other man have I seen such a capacity for devotion to a friend.' This statement about Bram was made after his death in 1912 by Hall Caine, the man who became his closest friend after he moved to London and to whom he dedicated *Dracula*. The Journal is replete with allusions to a number of friends and acquaintances from his years in Dublin, most of whom were associated with his time at Trinity College Dublin and, as we shall see, went on to become great achievers in their respective chosen careers.

Bram Stoker entered Trinity College in 1864, just a few weeks shy of his seventeenth birthday. In spite of his mysterious childhood illness, he was by the age of sixteen a healthy, strapping young man whose height and red hair made him conspicuous above the rest of the freshmen. Although he did not place highly on the Trinity entrance examination, the primary schooling and tutoring Bram had received was sufficient for acceptance.

Physically, Bram hit his stride during his Trinity years, demonstrating his versatility as well as his endurance by excelling in rugby, race walking, rowing and gymnastics. He represented the Trinity College Rugby Club between 1868 and 1871, his notable achievement being part of the 1st XV in 1868 that won all of its twenty-seven matches. Later he was honoured with caps for exceptional play and served on the organising committee. Winning a variety of prestigious race-walking events between 1866 and 1868, Bram collected many silver goblets and trophies. As race walkers are typically small and light framed, Bram's enormous strength and size would have been a handicap. Bram's versatility was also impressive. In June 1870 he excelled at a gymnastics event held at Trinity. He came in first in putting the 42lb weight and the 16lb shot, as well as slinging the 56lb and the 42lb weights. He also ranked first in the event combining the results of vaulting, high jump and the long jump with trapeze.

Bram also rowed for the Dublin University Boat

Club, participating in both the pairs and the fours events. In *Dublin University Boat Club Reminiscences*, Maj. M. P. Leahy remembers 'father Abraham Stoker … of Botany Bay' as one of the first to initiate him to the joys and sorrows of rowing. He further remembers that before his time, 'They rowed at Ringsend, mostly in choppy sea water, with planks, dead rats, and flotsam and jetsam of all kinds around them. The boats were frequently filled, and almost as frequently sank, in the choppy seas on which they performed.'

While at Trinity, he was also drawn towards intellectual and oratorical opportunities, including the prestigious Philosophical Society, an extracurricular group whose members focused on reading and discussing papers, ranging from aesthetics to politics and the supernatural, in-vogue topics on which to cut one's philosophical tooth and sharpen one's wit. In 1868, Bram read his ironically titled paper, 'Sensationalism in Fiction and Society'; other members read papers on subjects such as 'The supernatural as introduced by the English Poets' and 'The Demonology of Milton', with much discussion centred on *Faust*.

Stoker was a leader rather than a follower, distinguishing himself by serving as president of the 'Phil' during 1869–70, and in 1872 as the auditor of the equally esteemed College Historical Society, after having been both librarian and secretary of the 'Hist'. His auditorial address at the opening meeting of the 1872–3 session on 13 November 1872, 'The Necessity for Political Honesty', was the high point of his association with the 'Hist'. The platform contained far more dignitaries that usual; VIPs included Professor Edward Dowden, Sir William Wilde, Dr. George F. Shaw and the Lord Mayor of Dublin. Stoker's status as an outstanding Trinity and, indeed Dublin, personality was reflected in the larger than usual attendance; the college Dining Hall where it was held 'was thronged in every part by visitors and students. There was some good-humoured noise but the audience obeyed an injunction against party demonstrations.' In 1873, Bram was made an honourary member of the 'Hist' and remained active even after receiving his degree, until he moved to London in 1878.

During the six years of Bram's somewhat sporadic attendance at Trinity, supplemented by outside tutoring, his studies did not seem his priority. While perfecting his oratorical skills, his deep involvement with the two societies, and his many sports and athletics responsibilities – all the while working part-time at Dublin Castle as a civil servant – Bram managed to complete a Bachelor of Arts in 1870, followed by a Master's degree several years later. He thrived on perpetual motion, as though still trying to reconcile his years of confinement and immobility.

*"Dublin Castle Gate, between the Royal Exchange and Newcomen Bank" (Samuel Brocas)*

He had begun employment at Dublin Castle in 186 5. 'Dublin Castle' is somewhat of a misnomer; in Brar 's time there was none of the romance or glamour t ie name implies. Hardly a castle, it was in the 1800s, as it is today, a group of buildings around a courtyard. Eut a castle had been built in the thirteenth century, on a hilltop previously settled by the Vikings. Dub in Castle functioned as a military fortress, contributing to the stretches of stone walls surrounding Dublin, a d as a prison, treasury, courts of law, and the seat of English administration in Ireland for 700 years. Dublin Castle continues to operate today as both a tourist attraction and a major Irish government complex; it is also used for important State receptions and Presidential inaugurations.

Bram worked with the Department of Registrar of Petty Sessions Clerks in the Chief Secretary's Office, the office from which his father had retired. After ten years, he was promoted to Inspector of Petty Sessions, a position he held until his resignation in late 1878. Petty Sessions, the lowest level of court services in Ireland and equivalent to the district courts of today, met regularly in many small towns to handle minor criminal cases. Petty Sessions was one of the reforms that replaced the practice of certain magistrates holding court in their parlours, applying laws and punishments to suit their own interests with impunity.

The court sessions recorded by Bram were rife with irregularities, and the inequities of the system were contrary to all he had been brought up to value. To replace the inconsistencies lingering from court to court and to produce a standardised system of procedure, Bram combed meticulously through massive amounts of documented material that had gathered since the founding of the Petty Sessions in 1851. During his final year at Dublin Castle, he worked on what would be his first published book, *The Duties of Clerks of Petty Sessions in Ireland* (1879), a work he would later refer to as 'dry as dust'. This book, which served as a manual within the

Irish civil service until the early 1960s, represents ten years of Bram's life, and his own contribution towards improving life for the poor and uneducated in Ireland. Further, his work stands as a complement to his mother's efforts over the years to improve the lives of the unfortunate. The rigour helped Bram hone his skills for methodical attention to detail, which was fundamental to his narrative style, especially in *Dracula*.

EXCEPTIONS.

*Puppies.*

Puppies born after the 31st March do not require to be licensed till the following year.

*Law Advisers' opinion, 24th July, 1866.*

*Dogs Imported.*

Dogs imported after 31st March do not require to be licensed till the following year.

*Dogs on Shipboard.*

Owners of Dogs on board ship lying in harbour are not required to take out License.

*Law Advisers' opinion, 17th April, 1869.*

*A short segment from* The Duties of Clerks of Petty Sessions in Ireland *(1879)*

Bram also had several friends among his colleagues at Dublin Castle. Though his work was undoubtedly tedious, the Journal provides glimpses into more relaxed moments during dinners at the office (190, 191, 192). There is also a brief account of the raucous experiences of a delegation who attended an association meeting in London (193).

At this stage of his life it became obvious that Bram was capable of taking on huge responsibility and that he relished hard work. He naturally moved into a lead role in school, work, and play, and his relatives recognised that like many other Stokers, Bram derived an understated level of personal satisfaction from his achievements. While a student at Trinity College, he had to juggle his studies, extracurricular activities and his athletics at Trinity with the demands of his job at Dublin Castle (six days a week, with reduced hours on Saturday). Today, Bram would be regarded as a 'workaholic'.

During this time, Bram widened his circle of friends beyond former classmates and fellow employees. Especially influential were Sir William and Lady Wilde, whose elder son Willie was Bram's classmate at Trinity. The Wildes were a rather bohemian couple who lived on Merrion Square; they were colourful, and a bit more risqué than the elder Stokers might have liked for Bram's mentors. Sir William and Lady Jane, or 'Speranza' as she was known, were active in the push for social reforms. As such their paths crossed with Charlotte's who, in spite of her disapproval of their lifestyle, respected their dedication to improving the plight of Dublin's poor.

Bram was a regular guest at the gatherings hosted by Speranza, who had a great literary reputation as a poet and writer as well as a certain notoriety for her bawdy language and flamboyant dresses. Dr Wilde, also well respected as a writer, was famous as a physician. He had fathered at least three illegitimate children before his marriage, a son whom he educated and made his heir, and two daughters who were adopted by his brother and raised as Wildes. One of many stories that emanated from the parties at the Wildes was that of Rev. Charles Tisdall and Dr Thomas Beatty, as recorded in *Reminiscences of Sir Charles Cameron*: 'The reverend and the medical doctor had excellent voices. Their habit was to meet in Wilde's study and then ascend the stairs very slowly, singing a duet, to the drawing room.'

Stoker pays homage to William Wilde as storyteller by including one of his stories in his Journal (181). Collector and Stoker enthusiast John Moore offers this comment:

His reference to Sir William Wilde's narration of the Robbery of the Galway Mail offers evidence of Bram's interest in events surrounding the Irish Rebellion of 1798 – some of which are cleverly woven into his first novel, *The Snake's Pass*. I have in my library a copy of W. J. Fitzpatrick's *Ireland before the Union* inscribed by the author to Sir William Wilde. This is a yellowback publication with an attractive illustration of the actual Galway Mail Robbery on the front cover. This publication, a sequel to *The Sham Squire*, in which Fitzpatrick identifies the leading spies and informers, covers the period of the rebellion. Bram may very well have read/consulted this very copy in addition to Sir William's influential narration. Wilde and his wife, who had nationalist leanings, certainly would have. The rebellion proper culminated in the defeat of the French/Irish forces in the fall of 1798 and the wholesale execution of Irish officers and leaders. Numbered among these is Charlotte's ancestor Richard Blake who held a commission – an event Bram would also have been made aware of.

Stoker's years in Dublin were certainly marked by a plethora of social activities. A local society columnist recorded:

'He was an excellent "party" young man, and of course, had always heaps of invitations. He talked to the old ladies – got supper for half a dozen fair ones together, by diving his tall form hither and thither amongst the crowds about the tables – and, when he stood up to dance, had a way of making a charge, which effectually cleared a passage through the most thronged ball-rooms. Everybody made way for Stoker – his coming was like a charge of cavalry, or a rush of fixed bayonets – nobody dreamed of not giving way before him, and so he and his partner had it all their own way. How my heart used to jump in my dancing days when Stoker asked me for a waltz!' (qtd in Murray, p. 52)

Bram enjoyed having fun at the expense of others. Take, for example, the allusion in entry 174. This has a backstory, originating in a paper entitled 'Moral Insanity in Criminal Cases', delivered in 1863 at the Statistical and Social Inquiry Society of Ireland. This organisation included Abraham Stoker as a member and Charlotte as an associate member; in fact, that is where she presented a paper (also in 1863) entitled 'The Necessity for the States Provision for the Education of the Deaf and Dumb of Ireland'. The 'Insanity' lecture, apparently still a 'hot topic' in the mid-1870s when Bram wrote this entry, focused on the need to abolish capital punishment, because it could not be properly determined whether someone was insane or criminal. Surely the Stokers discussed the topic, and Bram's humourous take informs the entry.

Again we have the anecdote about Mrs Glover (194) passed along to Bram by G. Dolby. Julia Glover (1779–1850) was a popular Irish actress. Actually, she had just two sons: Edmund (an actor and theatre manager) and William Howard (a violinist who was a member of the Lyceum's orchestra) – but three made for a much better story!

## TRANSCRIPTIONS

### ⇢⇒ 166 ⇐⇠

*Magan, the College Skip,*[94] *told T. Trevor White*[95] *that during the vacation he had been on tour around the south of England. 'I did not go to France sir', said he, 'nor yet to Wales nor to Birmingham because I thought that the dialects would be against me.'*

27th of October, 1872

### ⇢⇒ 167 ⇐⇠

*Fire at Delany's in Westmoreland St.*[96]
   *Inquest servant's mother putting her hand into the coffin*

---

94   Skips were employees at Trinity College who performed basic culinary duties for the students.

95   T. Trevor White, a friend of Stoker's with a BA from Dublin, later became a solicitor in London.

96   A locally famous fire took place in June 1866 at the Delany home, near Carlisle (now O'Connell) Bridge. It claimed six lives, among them a servant. There was indeed an inquest. It was determined that the tragedy was compounded by chemicals present in the taxidermist's shop next door, lack of water pressure and faulty fire escapes. No charges were filed.

## JUNE.

7. DREADFUL FIRE WITH LOSS OF LIFE IN DUBLIN.—A most tragical fire occurred in Westmoreland-street, Dublin, in which no less than six persons lost their lives. The corner house of that street, adjoining Aston-quay, and just at Carlisle-bridge, had been recently rebuilt, and was occupied by the Ballast Board. The next house, numbered 19 and 20, was occupied by Mr. Delaney,

⇢ 168 ⇠

*Went down to the University Gymnasium today and there met Thornhill performing in the trapeze as usual. When he came off I took him to task for neglecting his College business & confining all his exertions to athletics. I said, 'Well Thornhill, I hear you never do anything nowadays at all except work on the trapeze.' He answered me quite gravely & seriously as one against whom an unfair imputation had been brought. 'Oh no I assure you. You must have been misinformed. I do a great deal – a very great deal on the horizontal bar.'*

2nd of May, 1873

⊸══ 169 ══⊷

*Dr Shaw[97] says: 'What man (beyond his brother in law[98]) affords to set a perfect example of the truth of Kant's philosophy. Kant you know says that: I walked with him the other day for only two minutes & it seemed to me that it was the longest unbroken period of time I ever remember – in fact it was a complete subjective phenomenon.'*

30th of August, 1873

⊸══ 170 ══⊷

### *Delany[99] Household & Menage*

*Servants room looking out through glass door on earth bank like side of grave with just room above ground to see a ghostly head against the moonlight creeping like shape Mrs D. digging in the garden like a ghoul.*

---

97   Dr Shaw (1821–1899) was a Junior Fellow at Trinity while Stoker was a student. He later became a member of the Governing Board of TCD.

98   Shaw's brother-in-law, George B. Wheeler, was an editor of the *Irish Times* and a writer of textbooks for Dublin schools.

99   Paul Murray indicates that an artist named Delany was Bram's housemate at one time. Whether this is the same person we do not know.

Abraham Stoker, Bram's father (1799–1876). For fifty years a dedicated civil servant, he shared his love of the theatre with Bram.

Charlotte (Thornley) Stoker, Bram's mother (1818–1901). An intelligent and strong-willed individual, Charlotte was an advocate for women's rights.

William Thornley Stoker, Bram's oldest brother (1845–1912). A medical doctor and president of the Royal College of Surgeons in Ireland, Thornley was knighted by Queen Victoria in 1895.

Matilda Stoker, Bram's older sister (1846–1920). An artist and author, Matilda was a member of Dublin's Royal Hibernian Academy, and studied painting and ceramics.

Thomas Stoker, Bram's brother (1849–1925). Educated at Trinity College, Tom served some thirty years in the Bengal Civil Service, before retiring to London in poor health.

Margaret Stoker, Bram's younger sister (1853–1928). At age twenty-five, Margaret married Sir William Thomson, surgeon and colleague of Thornley's, volunteered in social causes and supported the arts.

Richard Stoker, Bram's brother (1851–1931). In 1901, Richard and his wife Susan emigrated to Vancouver Island (Canada) where they established a vast rhododendron garden.

George Stoker, Bram's youngest brother (1854–1920). A medical doctor, George served in both the Russo-Turkish and Zulu Wars.

ABOVE Florence (Balcombe) Stoker, Bram's wife (1858–1937). This sketch was drawn by Frank Miles, a friend of Oscar Wilde and reputedly one of his lovers.

LEFT Noel Stoker, son of Bram and Florence (1879–1961). Educated at Summer Fields School, Winchester College and the University of Oxford, Noel became a Chartered Accountant and established his own firm in London.

Bram Stoker (1847–1912), sketch by unknown artist.

Inscription in the Bible given to Bram on his eleventh birthday.

Tankard awarded to Bram as Athletics Champion at Trinity College in 1867.

Service medals awarded to Major George Stoker.

THIS TABLET IS
ERECTED IN MEMORY OF
ABRAHAM STOKER ESQ
FOR 50 YEARS IN THE
IRISH CIVIL SERVICE,
DUBLIN CASTLE.
HE DIED AT
LA CAVA IN ITALY.
OCT. 12TH 1876. IN THE
78TH YEAR OF HIS AGE.
BELOVED AND RESPECTED BY
ALL WHO KNEW HIM FOR HIS
MANY AND GREAT VIRTUES.

Memorial to Abraham Stoker Sr, located at Church of Ireland, Rathfarnham.

⇥ **171** ⇤

*S. King complained that in settling the prelimi-*
*naries of his marriage, his fiancee's father seemed*
*to care only about his life being well insured as*
*if his immediate death was the only thing worth*
*caring about a reckoning on.*

⇥ **172** ⇤

### *Vengeance – Prompt & Complete*

*A. S.*[100] *'But if that theory be sound then any other*
*man would have as much right as you have to kiss*
*your wife.'*

    *Cornelius O'Callaghan:*[101] *'If I had a wife,*
*which I haven't, thank God – and caught any man*
*kissing her I don't know if I would have right;*
*but I know that I would have a poker. And in a*
*moment the poker would be on his skull, his brains*

---

100  Bram.

101  Most likely John Cornelius O'Callaghan, author of *History of the Irish*
     *Brigades in the Service of France* (1870) and supporter of the re-separa-
     tion of Ireland from the UK.

*on the floor, his body out of the window and his soul in Hell.' Said quickly & impromptu.*

17<sup>th</sup> of August, 1874

═ 173 ═

*Dr Shaw junior Fellow TCD was told that at a supper party of some friends of his the death of Dr Moore SFTCD was proposed – and an amendment carried, 'death & damnation'. 'No, no', said Dr S., 'I want no more than his death. Any more would be an embarrass de richesse.'*[102]

═ 174 ═

*Dr Shaw FTCD, 'Do you mean to tell me that Abraham not being a dangerous lunatic was about to kill his own son?'*

---

102   The cause of this resentment is unknown. Possibly it was a consequence of rivalry between a junior fellow and his more senior colleague (in other words, typical academic politics).

⇥═ 175 ═⇤

Murray: 'Ah now, Tyrrell.[103] I tell you what I'd do
    when I saw a fine girl at the flower show or
    such. I'd just go and buy a handsome watch and
    chain or some such thing & come up and slap it
    on to her and ask her to marry me.'
Tyrrell: 'But her father or brother might give you
    an impulse a tergo.'
Murray: 'And what for? Is it quarrel with me
    for giving a thing that cost a lot of money and
    asking to marry her at once. Not very likely?'

⇥═ 176 ═⇤

Miss K. did not hesitate in sending home gloves
from Brussels to put on the outside that they were
samples. She 'did not consider it a lie when it was
written in French'.

---

103  Robert Yelverton Tyrrell, three years older than Bram, was elected a
     Fellow of Trinity College in 1868. An advocate of Walt Whitman's poetry
     during the 1870s, he started a college miscellany, *Kottabbos*, in 1874.

*"Going to the Levee" 1897 (Rose Barton)*

*One day when there was a Levee at the Castle a lot of men were putting on their academicals to attend in the old robing room (called by some men robbing room at one time from some robberies of purses etc.) kept by Waters & Wilson close to the Examination Hall, and many cabs came to convey them away. One man was very late & the cabs had gone. A porter went to the gate & hailed to the 'hazard' and five or six cabs came. When they found that only one was wanted the baffled ones went away grumbling & larruped their horses standing up to do so. The one engaged stood on the steps warming himself in cabman fashion by beating across his chest with both arms and remarked to some men standing near. 'Well gentlemen, they oughtn't to mind. Shure we larn in the skripters that many is called but few is chose.'*

## ⚬= 178 =⚬

*Andrew Reed[104] was a very nice fellow but he was queer in the eyes. One moved restlessly whilst the other had a cold & stony glare. Thus whilst you were talking to him you were quite unhappy. One eye fixed you firmly, so firmly that you could not take your eyes off it whilst you knew that all the time the other eye was critically examining you from head to foot.*

## ⚬= 179 =⚬

*An enthusiastic gymnast said after having had a prolonged tour, 'I have hung by my feet from*

---

104 Andrew Reed (later Sir Andrew), born in Galway in 1837, served in the Royal Irish Constabulary and was appointed District Inspector and later Inspector General. Widely known as a very civil policeman, he authored *The Irish Constable's Guide* and *The Policeman's Manual.*

*every spire and done the hand balance on every communion rail in Europe.'*

#### ⇢ 180 ⇠

*E. T. K. said that Mrs C. 'seemed to be afraid of getting interested in anything'.*

#### ⇢ 181 ⇠

*The mail which used to go from Dublin to Ballinasloe & which just before every fair carried great quantities of notes, gold & bills was robbed about Enfield (Co. Meath) about 1840. Roger O'Connor[105] [King][106] was tried for the robbery and was acquitted there being no evidence. Some years afterwards [blank] son of [blank] was driving in the box of the coach from Dublin to Dunleary beyond Kingstown to catch the mail to England. He was very sprightly & began to 'chaff'*

---

105 For many years a prominent character in Irish affairs, he was involved in the revolutionary movement of the United Irishmen. In 1817 he was tried for complicity in the robbery of the Galway coach and murder of the guard, but was acquitted.

106 Descendant of the last High King of Ireland before the Norman invasion, O'Connor adopted the acronym ROCK (Roger O'Connor King).

*the driver who was tooling his team along steadily*
*& in silence. Jehu[107] took no notice.*

*'I seem to know your face my man. I've seen you*
*before.'*

*No notice.*

*'D'ye hear, we've met before my man – I seem to*
*know your face.'*

*The driver looked up.*

*'Yes your honour sir. I druv the coach that*
*night.'*

Told by Sir W. Wilde, 6th of February, 1876

⇒ 182 ⇐

*'Every man is living on every other man's back,*
*with his nails dug in.' C. Martelli*

⇒ 183 ⇐

*Horan and three other men once had lodgings*
*in Gardiner St. Lower.[108] They had taken them*

---

107  A slang term for a cab driver. Source is Jehu, an ancient king of Israel
known proverbially for his swift chariot driving.

108  William Horan, a solicitor, was living at 81 Gardiner St. Lower in 1862.

*by the quarter, but after a few weeks found that their landlady plundered them fearfully. To test this they opened a bottle of sherry & placed it in a cupboard & no one touched it. Still it got less & less till it was finished. Whole joints disappeared, etc. They then said they would not stay any longer and got other lodgings. The landlady told them she would not let them go & would if necessary pros-ecute for rent. They said very well & stayed.*

*They always breakfasted – dined out so that there was no plunder. They came home very late & one by one & each one knocked up the house. They gave bachelor parties lasting till 4 & 5 o'clock with dances. They gave musical parties with horns & a drum & got friends to call always for some of them when going home from parties at the small hours.*

*At the end of the second week the landlady implored them to go & offered to let them off the rent due.*

⋙ 184 ⋘

*At the little hotel we stopped in at Mountshannon Dec 75 (Corbet, Hennell & self), there was a*

---

Gardiner St. Lower, on the north side of the Liffey, was at that time popular for its boarding houses.

*very pretty buxom young maid servant who did all that we wanted well & quickly but whom we noticed never spoke a word. One night H. & I went into the kitchen to smoke & get feathers to clean our pipes. There was an immense heat hearth & several girls were present & all was jolly. H. asked for a feather & so the silent maid ran to a corner, lifted the lid of a box, took out a live struggling fowl & after pulling a handful of feathers from it put it back.*

*Presently we were chaffing the girls about marrying & asking what sort of husband they would like. Suddenly the silent maid turned round – she was washing dishes in a tub – & said quickly & decisively, 'Big min's the best', and then turned hastily & rubbed the plates. These were the only words we ever heard her speak.*

⇒ 185 ⇐

*H. wanted a 'Cutty' pipe well blacked & a good blackthorn stick. He bought one of each from a man & ever after everyone offered sticks & pipes for sale & as gifts. In one place a small child far away from any human habitation stood waiting barefoot in the snow to give his 'anr' a black pipe.*

*Jemmy Grey RHA*[109] *told story of old man Waters*[110] *a chicken butcher in Britain St.*

*When he gets drunk he always wants something to eat & begins to call his wife coaxingly – Catherine, Kate, Katey, Katty – & gradually gets less tender till he calls her an old w__. His wife looks him up & he shouts for food. 'In truth it's a bowl of soup or a pig's fut I'd like this night. I'm tearin' mad wid the hunger. In troth I could eat one of the ould gandhers in the yard. Bad luck to them bloody ould gandhers. They do be nourished daily and here's their masther sufferin' the pangs of hunger. Be [blank] if I could only git hould iv a match. I'd burn ould Katty in her roost. In troth it's myself that'll pathernise Tandstickor*[111] *this night.'*

### 3rd of March, 1876

---

109 Well-known Irish painter James Grey, member of the Royal Hibernian Academy, an artists' organisation that still exists. His father and three of his brothers were also artists.

110 John Waters, poulterer, lived on Great Britain St. in the Mountjoy area of Dublin.

111 'Tandstick' is Swedish for 'match'. Matchstick production was one of Sweden's major industries.

⌐═ 187 ═⌐

*On one occasion when very drunk he put 400 chickens into the [blank] on them.*

*One Xmas eve <xxx xxx> he said to J. G. 'Ah Misther Jem, come in here & see me Christmas fare.' He took him into the shop parlour & there lying in the fire half charred was a splendid prize goose tethered to the fender with a hay band round its neck. 'It's in there since two o'clock', said Waters.*

⌐═ 188 ═⌐

*T. Drew RHA*[112] *complained to the milkman of the quality of milk supplied & threatened to get Cameron,*[113] *the city analyst, to look into it. The man promptly told him that he didn't care a damn*

---

112  Most likely Thomas Drew who would become a leading Irish architect of his day. (Coincidentally, he designed the building at Trinity College Dublin that now houses the 'Bram Stoker Room'.)

113  Sir Charles Alexander Cameron was an Irish physician who for over thirty years was the Chief Health Officer in Dublin. He is reported to have cut the death rate from one of the highest in Europe to one of the lowest. This is likely the same Dr Cameron mentioned in entry 131.

*– that that bloody old Cameron might come &
tantalise the milk as much as he chose.*

### ⇒ 189 ⇐

*A man who was in prison (a carpenter) told T.
Drew when he came out that the skilly[114] was so
thin that 'it would run a mile down a rough deal'.*

### ⇒ 190 ⇐

*When there was extra work going on in a certain
office[115] in Dublin, many of the men used to come at
9 in the morning and stay till 9 at night, and being
in rooms where the public never entered, used to
cook their own dinners – under the supervision
of one senior clerk who himself did most of the
cooking. Strange dinners were arranged. It was a
common thing to eat a few snipe & some carrots
or parsnips. One day there was a big dinner. The
table was covered with a cloth made of sheets of
blotting paper gummed together. Eight sat down.
The dinner consisted of hare soup, a roast turkey*

---

114   A thin soup or gruel.
115   Maybe his own, in Dublin Castle.

stuffed with forcemeat (this was carved in a wash hand basin) two teal, several snipe, pota-toes, carrots, parsnips, turnips, salad, fried plum pudding, sherry, beer, champagne, moselle, port claret, curacon, a cup of coffee, punch.

There was a universal press in an inner room in which a couch could be made with old clothes. On one occasion the following dialogue took place (it was 13 February).

J. 'Is G. calmly slumbering in the press still?'

T. 'No, he has got up & lit his pipe & is writing a valentine.'

⊷ 191 ⊶

One man who used to buy the provisions would sometimes go out to market & return with a boy who bore an enormous basket of different kinds of meat, vegetables & birds & a few hares & rabbits. These were in common use – wild duck – teal – <xxx> – snipe – turkeys – widgeon – chickens etc.

One day when the men were talking of the differ-ent things which they had sent, the office messenger for A. said he had sent for a square of unleavened bread describing it as of the shape of a sarcophagus. The messenger returned without it & told him that at the bakers they had laughed at him & told him there was no such a thing in bread as a sarcopofalus. G. said that he had sent out for 5/- worth of postage stamps & had been brought back that value of ham sandwiches.

T. said, 'The strangest thing I ever sent him for was a dead dog.' Shouts of laughter. 'Well said, T. Here he comes.' And sure enough the messenger entered having brought from Sandymount[116] a large newspaper parcel which when opened was found to contain the corpse of a large mongrel dog – a pet which had just died & was going to the taxidermist.

$$\text{192}$$

On one occasion T. was pretending to spar with an imaginary opponent & was dancing about as if dodging imaginary blows & saying 'Ha! Would you', etc., a lot of his confreres looking on & encouraging him. The door opened & in came a grocer's man with a dozen of beer. T. did not see or hear him & all the rest were silent. T. still continued his contest in blissful ignorance till the man could no longer suppress his laughter.

---

116    Sandymount is a neighbourhood in southeastern Dublin.

*It was a common thing to get from a tavern a dozen of oysters in a bottle or a potted herring in an envelope. T. was very skilful in throwing half-pence into a kettle across a room.*

⟿ 193 ⟿

*In 1874 the Irish P. S. Clerks association sent a delegation of their members to London to try to aid in passing an Act which would be beneficial to them. There were six of them and in a fort-night they spent £300. Two of them spent a week of the time on a bend in Paris. One 'the man from Galway' wanted to take the whole female staff of the Westminster telegraph office which they used for a picnic to Richmond in acknowledgment of their service. They were the curse of the Irish office, being there morning noon & night. On the day of their interview with the Chief Sec. their spokesman was so drunk that they had to put him under a pump before going & even then his head was steaming like a wet furnace. Finally before leaving London they had a regular fight & several got black eyes & cut faces.*

*They left a pipe, a package of tobacco & a case of whisky at the Carlton Club[117] for an Irish official 'lest he should be lonely'.*

⊷ 194 ⊶

*'Mrs Glover 1781–1850'*

*G. Dolby[118] told me a story of Mrs Glover.*

*On one occasion – I think her birthday – Mrs Glover was seated after dinner with her three sons Edmund, William & Howard, all well grown boys. She said, 'Edmund my boy, here is your very good health and may you have all the virtues of your father. He was the finest tragedian ever lived & a perfect gentleman – Edmund Kean. And here is to your health William, and may you emulate in your life the many beauties of your father's character. He was the best comedian of his time and a perfect gentleman – William Farren. And Howard my boy, here is your health too and may*

---

117 An elitist conservative gentlemen's club in London.

118 George Dolby was Charles Dickens's secretary and manager from 1866 to 1870, during his reading tours in Great Britain and the United States. For a short period he also served as Mark Twain's agent.

*you too my youngest blossom shine as your father shone. He was – let me see, let me see – I have forgotten who he was, but I know – I know that he was a gentleman.'*

18<sup>th</sup> of December, 1876

—— 195 ——

'*There are other white garments for men to wear on earth besides the surplice.'*

BS

—— 196 ——

### *Mem*

*Crow's feet around eyes are footmarks of raven*
*1 for sorrow*
*2 for might*
*3 for a wedding*
*4 for a birth*

On the Bridge (15-9-78) several work people men & women
were talking. It was Sunday evening & some of them
sufficient liquor on board to make the giving of —
an easy matter. One woman had made an observ—
& a man had struck in—

"Now Mrs Murphy ye ought to be very careful how—
make any observation of that kind — Do ye know
its an insult to me & me wife"

"No I don't I know nothin' of the kind"

"Well ye oughtn't to insult us"

"Insult ye indeed — Whoisinsultin' yez or wants to
at all. Musha it's mighty often the ears of—
is open to insults this night. Troth an I'm t—
its little of insults you'll be hearin' when the
Divil looks at yez an' sez "Come".

Two drunken men were coming home by moonlight
as they got opposite to the lake. One said
"Paddy that's a fine moon"
He looked critically at the splendid sheen of the moonlight
with & said. "Yes Bygorra it is — a right good moon
so sudded. with drunken gravity "An' mind ye I'm hell hard to plea—

# SIX

# ⊷ THE STREETS ⊶
# OF DUBLIN

Founded in the ninth century, by Stoker's time the city of Dublin was well spread out on both sides (north and south) of the River Liffey. In 1800, its population had been about 180,000. Though the rest of Ireland underwent a dramatic decline in population during and subsequent to the famine of 1846–50, Dublin actually gained residents as many country folk flocked to the city to escape their misery. As a commercial and transport city, it offered employment in white-collar as well as unskilled and domestic jobs. In Stoker's day, however, there still was appalling poverty, with many of its most destitute relegated to workhouses. The city did gradually acquire a few amenities: the streets had gas lights (electricity would not make its first appearance until 1881), there were a few sewers, as well as a railway line and horse-drawn buses.

Bram Stoker was certainly familiar with the streets of central Dublin. In 1866 when he began work at Dublin Castle, he moved with his parents and two sisters from Upper Buckingham St. in north Dublin to Rathgar, a suburb of south Dublin. This meant that, like his father, he was faced with a long walk to work (about 4km) and back. It is doubtful whether Stoker (or his father before him) would have been able to regularly afford the luxury of a horse-drawn cab, and the Dublin tramways would not open until 1872. By 1871, the year he began his Journal, the family was on the move again, this time the remaining five of them piling in with their brother Thornley on Harcourt St. Fortunately for Bram, this was much closer to Dublin Castle. His walks would have offered a cross section of Dublin life and landscape as the shop fronts along Aungier St. gave way to the grandeur of the Royal College of Surgeons and the beauty of St Stephen's Green.

Now approaching the age of twenty-four, Bram had an active life: working, participating in events at Trinity College, serving as a theatre reviewer and frequently attending the Theatre Royal and later the Queen's Theatre and the Gaiety. With plenty of back-and-forth from one to the other, he had further opportunity to observe and record both visually and verbally a variety of 'street life'. That he took advantage of such opportunities is evident in the number of entries that focus on the streets of Dublin.

One striking feature of the Journal entries is Stoker's ability to observe and absorb details. From the outset, his writing shows a strong propensity for description. Take, for example, his description of the man on the ship who is off to go 'bushwhacking' in Australia (199) with his riding trousers, jack-boot leggings, and tunic with broad black leather belt. Stoker was attracted to the adventurous man, a type who inhabits some of his later fiction: Grizzly Dick in *The Shoulder of Shasta* (1895) and Elias P. Hutcheson in 'The Squaw' are mountain men; Harold An Wolf, hero of *The Man* (1905), returns from panning gold in Alaska; and Adam Salton, the hero of *The Lair of the White Worm* (1911) returns to England from Australia. The man on the ship in Dublin is carrying a bowie knife, certainly not a common object in Ireland (being a weapon of choice in frontier America). Of course, readers of *Dracula* will recall that the Count is killed with two knives, one of which is a bowie, wielded by Quincey P. Morris, a man of the American frontier.

Stoker recounts most of his anecdotes in a some-what detached manner. Even if he is part of the story, he distances himself from it, much as would a reporter. There are, however, exceptions. One example is the story of his encounter with the beggar woman on a Dublin street (198). He recalls this incident in some length, lingering over every detail. He allows his own emotions to show through, albeit briefly, while at the same time attempting to shape the story into appropriate prose. The cumulative effect of the sentences beginning 'No mistaking' distils the emotion into something significant and worth holding on to.

Arguably the strongest impression one gets while reading through the Journal is the 'Irishness' of much of the content. Not only is Stoker describing for the most part Irish scenes (both in Dublin and around the countryside), he presents them with typical Irish flour-ish. Many of the Dublin entries record humourous anecdotes, some personal – some second-hand. But while much of the humour is similar to what we noted in Chapter 3, there is a distinct difference.

Charles L. Graves, in 'The Lighter Side of Irish Life', writes: 'Humour is never more effective than when it emerges from a serious situation. Tragedy jostles comedy in life and the greatest dramatists and romancers have made wonderful use of this abrupt alternation' (p. 37).

Nowhere is the merging of tragedy and comedy more apparent than in Irish humour – and nowhere does Stoker employ it so pointedly than in the anecdotes from the Dublin streets. Irish history is rife with irony and incongruity, qualities which lie at the core of both tragedy and comedy. Ireland's history follows a repetitive pattern of downfall and recovery. Over the centuries it seems that before Ireland recovered from one pratfall, she was confronted with yet another round of famine, disease and oppression. Part of the resilience of the Irish lies in their ability to laugh at themselves as well as others. No one was above using humour; no subject was too sacred; no one was spared. Even when the situation is more futile than funny, Irish humour attempts to make light of dark.

The results are often grim and disturbing. Frequently it is a woman who is the butt of the joke. One such is the anecdote of the woman who judged the goodness of her husband by the fact that he had never given her a black eye (201). Other examples are scattered throughout: the woman who begged the pardon of a man she had struck, thinking it was her husband (206); the Club habitué's demeaning comments about women (212); and the woman who loses her breakfast after being kicked in the stomach (220). We can only wonder whether Bram actually found these incidents funny – and on what level – or if his interest was social commentary. We just do not know.

Similarly we have Frances Gerard's record of an episode at the St Patrick's Ball (208), an annual event held on 17 March, the climax of a day of festivities hosted by the Viceroy at Dublin Castle:

> A sort of general licence prevails, and the Chamberlain, that awful personage who holds in his hand the sesame to Castle festivities, relaxes for this night only his usually stern morality, and allows some pretty debutante who has not been presented to taste the joys of a private presentation which admits her to the halls of delight. Fast and furious grows the fun, and so too the flirtations, many a halting lover being helped over the bridge which separates flirtation from matrimony by the kindly influence of the patron saint, aided by the Viceroy's champagne. (Gerard, 'Picturesque Dublin', p. 19)

Attending with some friends, Stoker records the rather disgusting behaviour of the young men frolicking in the vomit in the centre of Leinster Hall (208). Even if he did not find it funny, the retelling of the story works as a joke – building up to a laughter-inducing punch line.

Violence is invariably linked to drinking and drunkenness. It is not known whether Stoker was at this stage of his life a drinker, though as noted earlier he was well known as a 'party man'. Certainly if his early fiction is any indication, he had great reservations about alcoholic consumption and the domestic violence that could ensue. His earliest work of fiction, *The Primrose Path* (1875), deals specifically with alcoholism ('the curse of Ireland') and the inevitable domestic violence that develops from heavy drinking. It reads like a tract for temperance.

Another prominent feature of many of the entries (and indeed his published writing) is the recreation of local dialect, accent and idiom. Rendering speech in dialect is a double-edged sword. On the one hand, it adds to realism, often a desired goal for a writer, especially one of supernatural fiction. Such local colour aids the reader in the 'willing suspension of disbelief'. On the other hand, it can test the patience of the reader, especially one completely unfamiliar with the dialect. Rendering dialect in written prose involves phonetic spelling of what is heard. This presents difficulties, of course, for the untrained ear – and slows the reading process.

Even more critical is the fine line between representation of realistic speech and negatively stereotyping the locals. A reader might even sense a class-consciousness, whether it is intentional or not. It sets up a distancing mechanism between teller of the anecdote (in some cases Stoker, in other cases a second-hand source) and those who speak in dialect (invariably less educated and frequently from the lower classes). Whether Stoker felt this way (as a university graduate, a civil servant he may very well have) we do not know. He obviously was proficient in the Queen's English – in the spoken as well as the written word – and most likely expunged from his own speech any idiom and localisms. But after he moved to England, he did retain his accent: 'For twenty-seven years he remained [in London] as private secretary to Irving – but he never lost his Dublin accent!' (*Irish Times*, 16 April 1938).

Then there are changes in grammatical structure common in Irish speech: 'they do be havin' to sit' and 'What would I be after doin'.' Other examples include 'am't' for 'am not', 'I seen' for 'I saw', and 'me' for 'my'. One also finds deviation from standard pronunciation, as in 'tirty' for 'thirty' and 'dat' for 'that'. A certain rhythmic lyricism can be detected in corruptions such as 'he sez, sez he' and 'at all at all'. All of these phrases and pronunciations can still be heard in Ireland today.

Another factor is the means of transmission. Most of these anecdotes that employ dialect are even more effective when spoken than when read, with accent and idiom adding to the humour. Possibly, as a public speaker of some note, Bram interspersed his talks with some of them. At the very least, he shared them in private conversations with friends and acquaintances. From comments made by some of his contemporaries, we know that Stoker was much more genial than his photographs and portraits suggest, not the humourless man that many assume him to have been. No doubt he embellished some of the tales, aware of the oratorical possibilities. Such a skill would be most advantageous for him later as Henry Irving's manager.

## TRANSCRIPTIONS

### ⟀ 197 ⟀

*Saw two queer things today. The first was a honey-seller – drunk. He was reeling along, yet with a wonderful instinct the dish of honey kept balanced on his hands. The second was a carpenter's boy with a sack of tools slung over his shoulder & an auger, the point of which projected about two feet in front of him. He had a frightful squint and in trying to avoid sticking each person he met, his obliquity of vision nearly succeeded in each case in doing that which he wished not to do.*

22nd of September, 1871

I was walking along quickly hurrying home to dinner when I was stopped by a woman who stepped out from behind the corner of the railing as I passed. The street was quite quiet & no one seemed to be in it but ourselves. The woman had a small roll of rough cloth – as a rubber in her hands (no professional beggar ever carries such a thing). I was not attending to anything but my own thoughts when I heard her voice. 'Oh sir, will you assist a poor body that wants help sorely.' (I quote her exact words as I remember every word she said and how she said it.) I stopped for I had passed her whilst she was speaking. I was feeling in my pocket for a penny when she came up. 'Sure it's dying of the shame I am at having to ask for anything. I that never took a half penny since I drew the breath of life.' No mistaking her want. No mistaking the tearful eyes that seemed too worn out to weep. No mistaking the clean labour-roughened, skeleton-like, trembling hands. No mistaking the tone of just-conquered independence in the quavering voice. No mistaking the wistful, supplicating, timorous attitude of one who could not cry and to beg was ashamed. I thought she wanted more than a penny and was *looking for a sixpence but a shilling turning up I gave it to her. She gave a low cry as she saw it fall into her hand – a low quick startled cry that almost wrung my heart, it contained such a woeful story. And then she burst out in prayer. I only heard the words 'Oh, may the good Lord never –' as I hurried away. That low cry was the sweetest & most plaintive music I ever heard in my life.*

3ʳᵈ of October, 1871, 10½ PM

⤳⇒ 199 ⇐⤶

*Saw Godkins (Marie & Ina)[119] off to St Remo tonight by Liverpool steamer from North Wall[120] at 8. On board was a youth evidently going to 'bushwhack' in Australia. He was walking about deck in*

---

[119]  Marie and Ina (Georgina) Godkin were the daughters of Irish author and journalist James Godkin. Their brother, Edwin Lawrence Godkin, was a newspaper editor after whom the Harvard University lectures were named. Marie and Ina spent several years living in Italy, after which Ina wrote *Life of King Victor Emmanuel II, First King of Italy* as G. S. Godkin, confusing reviewers who assumed she was Mr Godkin.

[120]  North Wall, the departure point of steamers and packets plying the waters between Dublin and Liverpool, was the scene of busy wharves, docks and warehouses.

*the following dress. White leather riding trousers with big jack-boot leggings. Tunic with broad black leather belt with suspended from it an enormous flask leather-cased, a pair of revolver holsters, bowie knife, bush cutlass, etc. & broad soft white felt hat.*

AS 12<sup>th</sup> of October, 1871

&#8594;&#8658; 200 &#8656;&#8592;

*Was walking across Carlisle Bridge[121] with T. M. M. We had been talking about pretty girls and I was remarking, 'It is wonderful how few nice look-ing girls you meet that are worth talking to; and also how girls change – every time you meet them they are getting quite different. There's a girl pass-ing that I met last winter when she had just come out. Now she looks like an old woman.' He said half angrily half jocosely, 'Why can't they remain as they are, what right have they to change?' I laughed but just then two persons passed us – an*

---

121    Carlisle Bridge, renamed in 1924, is now O'Connell Bridge. Built in 1790, Carlisle Bridge was in Stoker's day a popular meeting place, as it was the most frequented passage between the northern and southern parts of Dublin. It also offered (and still does offer) outstanding views of the city.

*old man and a little boy. The old man (not very old but middle-aged) was trembling all over and his knees knocked together as he walked, although he seemed a hale strong man. The boy looked flurried too and was holding him by the hand & directing him across the crossing. The faces of both were dirty, smeared with dirt and sweat & dust and tears; and the man bore on his shoulder a coffin about five feet long. I stopped laughing & thought.*

3rd of April, 1872

*A plaque on O'Connell Bridge (formerly Carlisle Bridge) Dublin*

201

*Heard an old woman in the street say to another woman, 'Aye indeed Biddy he was always the good husband to me. All the years I was married to him he never once gave me a black eye.'*

8th of September, 1873

⟶ 202 ⟵

*Two medical students quarrelling with a man who had broken a bone of each, not for his ill deed or their pain but for injuring their skeletons.*

⟶ 203 ⟵

*At wedding 14/7/74 one girl (bridesmaid) was left in the church. Five militia captains rushed into one carriage to avoid her & left her to come home alone. Was also left in the supper room at ball. Fancy the driver of the carriage feeling the insult & himself included in it & angry with the girl & whipping up his horses standing up to do so & bring them up at a gallop.*

⟶ 204 ⟵

*At the Lord Mayor's banquet the ice spoons ran short. One man of resource eat his ice with his eyeglass.*

### ⇢⊶ 205 ⊷⇠

*In very poor neighbourhoods there seem to be very many barbers and yet no one is ever either brushed or cut or shaven except the barbers themselves.*

### ⇢⊶ 206 ⊷⇠

#### *'Wifely Affection'*

*The barber asked the little hunchbacked man whom he was shaving how he got the horrible cut on his head which was not yet healed. He replied. (This was heard by H. T. De Burgh)*[122]

*'Well now I'll tell ye. The other day as I was goin' down the street as I was passin' Mrs Cassidy's door I heerd a yellin' an' a bawlin' an' the little girl came runnin' out an' ses she, 'Mr Murphy', ses she, 'will ye come in will ye oh do. They're murderin' me ma.'*

*'Well Mary me child', ses I, 'I'll not see them murderin' your ma', an' wid that I went in.*

*When I got into the room there was Mrs Cassidy wid her hair all down an her face as red as blazes an'*

---

122    Hubert T. De Burgh was a fellow student at Trinity College.

*her married daughter an' another girl houldin' her an' she was screechin' awful. An' the moment I kom in she gave a terrible screech an' she ses, ses she, 'Let me at him', ses she an' she ran at me holdin' the bellows in her hand by the nozzle an' she hit me over the skull.*

*An' when I kom to me senses the first thing I seen was me blood upon the ceilin'. An' there was Mrs Cassidy bendin' over me and when she saw me sensible she ses ses she, 'Oh Mr Murphy shure I beg your pardon. I thought it was me husband.'*

*Well I thought I was kilt entirely an' oh boys Jewel wasn't there. Cashins of blood all over the flore an' me head was like a well with the blood runnin'.*

*They took me home in a cab and me wife washed me in two tubs of water an' they was like tubs of blood. An' then I wint to the docther an' he examined me very careful and ses I, for I was mighty anxious intirely, 'Dr Jewel', I ses ses I, 'Will I die?' And he looked at me an' he ses ses he, 'Ye will.'*

*An' then my wife began to yell & bawl till the police kem kickin' up a shindig at the hall dure – and ses the docther ses he, 'Will ye hould your whistle,' ses he, 'Do ye want to ruin me intirely? Yes', he ses, 'ye will die but not of this.'*

[Marg: Heard by Hubert de Burgh]

### ⇢ 207 ⇠

*Common expression in Dublin for going on a 'spree' was to 'turn the slate'. It arose from the fact that in the days when wakes were common, anyone who wanted to go to one used to go to some coffin makers in Cork where all the coffin makers lived and looked on the slate hung up inside the door whereon the orders were written.*

### ⇢ 208 ⇠

*St Patrick's Ball for the Irish People in the Exhibition Palace[123] 187_ Admission 1/- Reserved portion 2/6*

*T. Martelli, Latchford,[124] self went. There were thousands of people there and all the brass bands in Dublin. Late in the evening many men got drunk & some sick. One man got sick in the centre of Leinster Hall. The floor was waxed. Immediately a lot of fellows with one impulse rushed at the place*

---

123  Exhibition Palace was converted in 1874 to a building that now houses the National Concert Hall.

124  Thomas W. Martelli and Henry Latchford were fellow students at Trinity College.

and cut a slide. It was awful. You might see shortly after a man being brought over from the bar to get sick in the right place for the continuance of the pastime.

W. Leahy who was very obstinate would not get out of the way of a trades band which was marching up & down so they knocked him down & walked over him. The last thing he heard was, 'Hit him with the fleuwtes. Hit him with the fleuwts.'

⋆⋅✦ 209 ✦⋅⋆

Dr Stokes was coming home late one wet evening along St Stephen's Green[125] when he saw & heard a solitary fiddler playing horribly out of tune on an execrable old fiddle. He stopped, & after a pause said –

'That's very bad music, my friend.'

The man stopped playing suddenly – looked at him in amazement & said, 'Oh the divvle a worse' & went on playing as fast as he could.

---

125  St Stephen's Green became a park in the late eighteenth century. Access was restricted to local residents until 1877 when it was opened to the public. The cost of its layout was paid for by Sir A. E. Guinness. Today the Green is one of Dublin's most famous and popular sites.

⊷⇛ 210 ⇚⊷

*An old beggar woman was asking alms of a well-known Orangeman[126] who repulsed her and when she persisted told her to go to Hell.*

*'To Hell?' she screamed. 'Is it to Hell ye mean. Arrah what would I be afther doiun' there – with the place as full of prodestans that they do be havin' to sit with their a\_\_s out on the windy stools.'*

⊷⇛ 211 ⇚⊷

*Two married men were standing at the gate of TCD looking at the crowds coming out. One of them after inspecting a lot of pretty girls said to the other, 'I say B., don't you think you & I would look well with the crape[127] up to the top of our hats.'*

---

126  The Orange Order (Orange Lodge) was founded in Loughgall, Co. Armagh in 1796. A Protestant fraternal organisation, it was based mainly in the north of Ireland and in Scotland.

127  'Crape' derives from the French 'crépe' – a fabric of gauzy texture having a crimpy appearance.

⇥ 212 ⇤

*The Club habitué said, 'Woman sir is essentially bad & worthless. She is only fit to give pleasure to some men between the ages of 20 & 50: and when a man becomes an old fool she takes care of him.'*

⇥ 213 ⇤

*An old dirty – exceedingly dirty shoemaker who comes up to my office to bring work for some of the fellows tells us stories in his own fashion. One of these was of a gentleman in Dublin whose wife died & he gave her a fine funeral. Shortly after he married again but before he had paid the bill for the first funeral the second wife died. The widower gave the second job to another house and the original undertaker billed him forthwith for the first. The bill was not at once paid & accordingly the discon-solate widower was summoned to Quarte sessions. The chairman said that the case was a scandalous one & asked the undertaker why he brought the action at such a time. To which he replied 'There an if he had trusted me with the second I would not have said a word of it at all at all for three years but he injured me character an' me thrade* when he wint the second time an' got goods from another house.'

The same old man described an outfitting shop in Thomas St as 'one where they'd equip you straight away with an outfit – complete an' all – a hat & a watch & a shirt & a coat & a purse an' a coffin'.

He also told of a lame attorney that came into him to blow him up about some delay in sending home his work. 'So I sez nothin' for a long time an' I let him bile away & then I sez, "Are ye done?" an' he sez, "Yes", sez he. Then sez I, "ye oughtn't to have the hard word for a shoemaker", I sez, sez I. "Why not?" sez he. "Because", sez I, "all the cripples in Ireland" sez I, "is made into shoemakers and attorneys", sez I. An' shure I thought he was going to knock me brains out with his crutch. An shure enough gentlemen it's a most strange thing that shoemakers is all family pets an' darlin's. Masons an' hatters and labourin' men and counsellors an' judges an' porters and the polis is all common childhern but I never knew an auld cobbler that wasn't the pet of the family.'

*The Dublin streets (1877) were in an unusually bad state of mud & the public were indignant with the corporation.*

*One morning a woman appeared in the police court before Mr O'Donnell & asked for help. She said her husband had deserted her. 'What is your husband?' asked the 'Beak'.*

*'A scavenger, your honour's worship.'*

*'Oh I see poor woman, poor woman. It is sad to be a widow.'*

*'But your honour's reverence's worship I amn't a widdy.'*

*'Oh yes you are, poor woman poor woman.'*

*'But your honour's worship. I take me God to witness that it's a decent married woman I am & not a widdy at all at all.'*

*'Oh you must be a widow, poor poor woman.'*

*'But your honour's holiness –'*

*'Pray cease my good woman. You really ought not to make such statements.'*

*'Your honour's –'*

*'Did you say your husband was a scavenger?'*

*'Shure an I did your worship & it's deserted me he has done.'*

'Then he is dead.'

'But he isn't dead but is livin' with that spawn of Hell Katey Flynn auld dirty Kate he is.'

'And really now my good woman, your husband is alive & a scavenger.'

'Yes! Your honour's worship.'

The 'Beak' carefully put on his spectacles & looked round the Court. 'Well I do declare', he said, 'that is the strangest thing I ever heard. Here is a woman who solemnly declares that her husband is a live scavenger. Woman I don't believe a word you say. There hasn't been such a person in Dublin for years.'

↔ 215 ↔

At the gate of the Lower Castle yard there is a sentry & round the gate cluster a number of work girls from Dollards[128] etc. at dinner hour & look at & be looked at by the sentry. On the gate is a placard beginning 'Wanted fine young men' (enlistment for artillery). The sentry was looking at the girls & holding his rifle at arm's length slanting. A blind man was coming along guided by a dog. One

---

128   Dollards Printing House (Dublin).

*of the girls in looking at the soldier unconsciously dropped part of her dinner from a paper. The dog started forward & dragged the blind man with his chin on the point of the bayonet.*

NB. This is a lie.

⟶ 216 ⟵

*"The General Post Office and the Pillar, Sackville Street Dublin"*
*(Thomas Sautell Roberts)*

*In Sackville St.*[129] *the North Dublin trams start from Nelson's Pillar*[130] *at the lower end and at the other end near the Rotunda*[131] *is a cabman's shelter. One evening an old lady got into the shelter*

---

129  Sackville St. is now O'Connell St.

130  Erected in 1808, Nelson's Pillar was blown up by the IRA in 1966.

131  A maternity hospital on Parnell St., still operational.

intending to go home by the last train & mistaking the place she stayed there two hours & refused to go, taking the admonitions of the jarvie for chaff.

⇢═ 217 ═⇠

An English officer used to tell his friends that when he was quartered in Dublin, he was once dancing with a girl at a Lord Mayor's ball. She said to him, 'Captain, dear. Ye must have throd on something or maybe it's only yer breath.'

⇢═ 218 ═⇠

On the Bridge several work people, men & women, were talking. It was Sunday evening & some of them had sufficient liquor on board to make the giving of offence an easy matter. One woman had made an observation & a man had struck in.

'Now Mrs Murphy, ye ought to be very careful how ye make any observations of that kind. Do ye know that it's an insult to me & me wife.'

'No I don't, I know nothin' of the kind.'

'Well ye oughtn't to insult us.'

'Insult ye indeed – who's insultin' yez or wants to at all at all. Musha it's mighty open the ears *of yez is open to insults this night. Throth an' I'm thinkin' it's little of insults you'll be hearin' when the Divil looks at yez an' sez "Come".'*

15th of September, 1878

→ 219 ←

*One Saturday night as I was going along Stephen's Green, I overtook the usual Saturday night group – artisan, wife & baby with marketing in a large basket. I overheard the following conversation:*

*Husband (stopping): 'Oh Mary, I forgot to tell ye – I seen me sisther today & she sez she's comin' to see us tomorrow.'*

*Wife: 'Well I'm shure an' we'll make her welcim.'*

*'But she'll stop for her dinner.'*

*'Well I'm shure, she'll be welcim as the flowers of May.'*

*'But what'll ye give her for dinner?'*

*'Now never you mind. She'll dine well.'*

*'But what'll ye give her?'*

*'Musha bad luck to your curiosity. Shure an' it's a tasty dinner I'll give her.'*

*'But what is it?'*

*'Oh now, don't be too curious. It'll be tasty.'*

'I'm not curious. What'll it be?'
'Well some bacon & a bit of ham.'

→🔘 220 🔘←

In Castle St. Dublin two women were talking. One was young & had a baby in her arms & was crying. The other, an old woman, was trying to comfort her.

'Musha it's the bad used woman ye are entirely. Maybe if ye was like poor Mrs Dunphy you'd have cause to be growlin' out iv ye.'

'Why? Who done anything to her?'

'Her man.'

'Well what did he do?'

'This woman, she hardly had the good breakfast into her body till she gets a kick in the stummick that sent it all up again.'

I Woodhouse told me he once went into a d[…] theatre in a back street in Wexford. The place was lit by tallow candles. & he & two friends we[re] the only persons in the boxes The play was [?] Helen being far gone in the way. all was so fu[…] that the party could not help laughing so much that Rob Roy came down to the footlights and asked them what they were laughing at – and by asking them (seriously) If they would like a[n] other play better for that in such case would be proud & happy to produce it a[…]

Barrowcliff

I once saw in the Queens Theatre a cork thrown [in] the orchestra by some wag in the gallery. He who was very drunk stood up stopped the band & mad[e] oration in which he called the audience in the gal[lery] assassins. He said holding up the cork "It was on[ly] accident & none of your fault that there was not [a] bottle at the end of it."

# SEVEN

# ⊷THE THEATRE⊶

Bram Stoker's attraction to the theatre predates the Journal. During his earlier years, his father encouraged this interest, taking young Bram to numerous productions and spending hours discussing with his son the actors, the sets and the performances. A great admirer of the actor Edmund Kean, Abraham Sr was able to boast that he had seen all of Kean's Dublin performances. On many occasions Bram went along with him, continuing this practice even more so after his father's retirement in 1865. The two of them – father and son – would sit in the pit, where the ticket prices were in line with their finances. Paradoxically, Bram's father never approved of the theatre as an occupation worthy of any of his sons.

During his years at Trinity College, Bram actually tried his hand at acting with the Trinity Dramatic Society, appearing in two Richard Brinsley Sheridan comedies, *The School for Scandal* and *The Rivals*. His professor and mentor, poet and Shakespearean scholar Edward Dowden, further inspired his interest in Shakespeare, whose plays would have a significant influence on *Dracula*.

In 1871, soon after he began writing entries in his Journal and a few months before his father left Dublin to live on the Continent, Bram approached the proprietor of the *Dublin Evening Mail* about writing theatre reviews. The response was that the paper could not afford such a thing, to which Bram replied that he 'would gladly do it without fee or reward'. And he did – for several years. This decision proved auspicious, as it began a chain of events that would result in his close association with Henry Irving, an eventual move to London, and a climate in which the writing of *Dracula* would be possible. Thus from little acorns do great oaks grow.

As a reviewer Bram had a free hand, with no editorial interference, and with no byline, the freedom to express himself anonymously. His reviews began appearing in late November 1871, just a couple of weeks after his twenty-fourth birthday. He is credited with introducing a major change in the way reviews were submitted and published in newspapers. Because of an early deadline, a newspaper review was destined to wait two days before appearing. At Bram's urging, the *Dublin Evening Mail* moved the deadline time back, allowing next-day publication, a benefit to both the cast of a play and other potential attendees.

Though Bram Stoker remained in his civil service job, he became even more active in the theatre and as far more than a reviewer. Accounts show that he frequented Dublin's main theatres – the Theatre Royal, the Gaiety and the Queen's – not merely as a member of the audience and/or reviewer, but as a backstage guest. During this time, he learned all he could about the inner workings of a performance: the lighting, the costumes, the staging, and offered advice and encouragement to young actors and actresses.

The first theatre reference in the Journal is a quotation from prominent Irish dramatist, Dion Boucicault (221). In *Personal Reminiscences of Henry Irving*, Bram repeats the statement about national drama, adding that Boucicault had a 'beautiful Irish brogue which was partly natural and partly cultivated' (vol. 1, p. 138). Bram also reviewed one of Boucicault's plays (*The Streets of London*) for the *Dublin Evening Mail* in April 1872. What is most interesting about Boucicault, however, is that one of his most popular plays was *The Vampire:*

*A Phantom Related in Three Dramas*. It is reasonable to assume that Stoker was familiar with this play.

*Henry Irving as Hamlet*

Theatre life was (and still is) fodder for numerous stories and anecdotes. Bram, just starting to get his feet wet as a writer, indulges in a few of his own, recording them with a humourous flourish: the artillery officer, the 'poker' and the 'pokee', and the drunken cork-launcher (227, 228, 230). Such anecdotes are not confined to Dublin. Bram tells a story about Frank Seymour, one of Cork's most colourful characters (231). Manager of the Victoria Theatre, he was usually in financial difficulties. Furthermore, he was a very poor actor. His nickname was 'Chouse' because of the way he pronounced the word 'chaos'. When he would be listed for a dramatic appearance, word would spread around Cork that 'Chouse has come again!' His creditors once posted bailiffs at the entrance to the theatre when he was to appear as the ghost in *Hamlet*. He avoided them by entering the theatre concealed in Ophelia's coffin.

The most significant of the theatre entries are those that mention Henry Irving (232, 233, 234, 235). Bram first saw Irving perform as Captain Absolute in *The Rivals* at the Theatre Royal in Dublin in 1867. Having seen him on stage again in 1871, Bram was discouraged by the lack of attention given to theatrical performances in the Dublin newspapers. That was his primary motivation for offering his services as theatre reviewer. In November 1876, Irving invited Stoker to join him at the Shelbourne Hotel after reading the astute observations the latter had made in two reviews of *Hamlet*. Brian J. Showers, author of *Gothic Dublin*, outlines the reviews:

> In the first review Stoker declared Irving 'the Garrick of his age' – a significant comparison to the legendary eighteenth century actor David Garrick, also noted for a defining turn as Hamlet. '[A]nd so', Stoker continues, 'we shall judge him by the highest standard which we know.'
>
> Stoker goes on to address two main points: the conception of character and its rendering. 'Mr Irving's conception is undoubtedly that of a thoughtful,

loving student of his author and his art. It bears evidence of thoughtfulness, of patient, minute scholarly attention, and of a rare thoroughness.' And in the rendering of the character, Stoker saw that 'The great, deep, underlying idea of [Irving's] Hamlet is that of a mystic.' According to Stoker, a further point that pleased Irving was the observation that 'To give strong grounds for belief, where the instinct can judge more truly than the intellect, is the perfection of suggestive acting'. (*Personal Reminiscences*, vol.1, pp. 26–7)

Stoker's assessment was no mere idolatry. As he himself later observed, 'There were plenty of things in my two criticisms which could hardly have been pleasurable [to Irving]' (p. 27). Among these was his criticism of Irving's weak physique: 'There is a variance between voice and gesture, or expression, which is manifestly due to want of physical power.' He also noted that Irving's 'voice lacks power to be strong in semitones'.

However, Stoker lauded the penultimate scene in which Hamlet kills Claudius: 'There is a realism which no one but a histrionic genius can ever effect.' In the end he judged Irving not as a common actor, but as a true artist.

Perhaps this combination of sensitive criticism and genuine honesty caused Irving to see in Stoker not only a new business manager, but also a true and sympathetic soul.

Soon afterwards the two met again. This time Irving presented the group (including Bram) with a dramatic reading of Thomas Hood's poem 'The Dream of Eugene Aram', a melodramatic tale of greed, death and retribution. 'So great was the magnetism of his genius', wrote Bram later of Irving's performance, 'so profound was the sense of his dominance that I sat spellbound.' At the end of the reading, Irving collapsed. Bram was overpowered by 'something like hysterics'. He readily succumbed to Irving's power. He had found a friend: 'Soul had looked into soul! From that hour began a friendship as profound, as close, as lasting as can be between two men.' At the end of the evening, Irving presented his new friend with a photograph inscribed: 'My dear friend Stoker. God bless you!' (*Personal Reminiscences*, vol. 1, pp. 29, 31, 33).

In the year that followed, Bram Stoker actively promoted Irving, including the organisation of a University Night in his honour. When Irving returned to Dublin in 1878, he shared with Bram his plan for a new theatre in London and invited his new friend to join him. Bram joined Irving as business manager of the Lyceum Theatre in December 1878; he remained in Irving's employ until the actor's death in 1905. In his own lifetime Bram Stoker was far better known as Irving's manager than as an author (even of *Dracula*).

The first reference to Irving in the Journal (232) is, coincidentally, in connection to performances of *Hamlet*. On the same page, Bram also records an incident that must be any actor's greatest fear: having nobody show up for a performance (233)! The other two entries provide comical anecdotes about another local 'character' – this time David Cunningham of Belfast, a man worthy of a Sheridan play (234, 235).

The influence of theatrical life, from these early encounters to the grand years at the Lyceum, can be strongly detected in much of Bram Stoker's writing. Allusions abound in many of his short stories and much of his non-fiction centres on the dramatic arts. Most significantly, *Dracula* itself owes much of its shape and power to its author's theatrical experiences. During the course of the novel, ten Shakespearean plays are referenced with several directly quoted. The play that most frequently resonates is *Hamlet*. Harker, having spent a long night with Dracula discussing Transylvanian history and the Count's ancestry, realises that he is a prisoner in the Castle. As morning approaches, Dracula ends his memoirs and Harker breaks off his diary 'like the ghost of Hamlet's father' (p. 31). In another early scene, Harker undergoes an unsettling experience: an encounter with the three vampire women in Dracula's Castle. Recalling the event, he questions his sanity and exclaims, quoting Hamlet, 'Tis meet that I put it down' (p. 37). Here he expresses the sentiments of many of the narrators of *Dracula*, who record their thoughts, feelings and actions in order to deal with anxiety: Mina Harker, Dr Seward, Van Helsing, even the captain of the ship that transports Dracula to England. Indeed, the writing and compiling of manuscripts becomes the means of self-preservation, as the collective effort of narration makes the defeat of Dracula possible.

Evidence of the influence of stage production on the text of *Dracula* lies in the theatricality of both lines and gestures. Both Henry Irving and Count Dracula are actors, practitioners of grand deceptions, both are shape-shifters who enter another role with ease, who blur the boundaries between illusion and reality. The grand sweep of Dracula's gestures mimics Irving in his finest roles – as Macbeth, as Lear, and especially as Mephistopheles (in *Faust*): 'You think to baffle me, you – with your pale faces all in a row ... My revenge is just begun! I spread it over centuries, and time is on my side' (*Dracula*, p. 315). Other examples come to mind: Dracula stretching out his arm to calm the wolves, crawling face-down down his castle wall, and forcing Mina to drink from the wound in his chest. Or this scene: 'With a fierce sweep of his arm, he hurled the woman from him, and then motioned to the others, as though he were beating them back ... "How dare you touch him, any of you? How dare you cast eyes on him when I had forbidden it? Back, I tell you all! This man belongs to me!'" (p. 40).

Without the theatre – and Bram's intimate connections with it – the novel *Dracula* as we know it would never have been written.

## TRANSCRIPTIONS

### 221

*'The reason why national dramas are always failures is because an audience should never come to a theatre with their sentiments in their pockets.'*

**Dion Boucicault**[132] **in conversation, 20th of April, 1872**

### 222

*Actor's use of charming – charming-notice*

---

132  Dion Boucicault (1820–1890) was in Dublin in April 1872 for performances of one of his plays (*The Streets of Dublin*).

*Two things about actors amuse me essentially. All actors and actresses speak of a notice which 'butters them up' as a charmingnotice. They run the two words into one from habit. And minor actors, chiefly men who have practically failed in their profession, always pride themselves on being 'a quick study' – verily being a quick study in the dramatic world is what in the commercial world is the lowest pitch of honest degradation – taking orders for salt.*

27<sup>th</sup> of October, 1872

···⇒ 223 ⇐···

*A funny thing occurred to me tonight. I was on the stage Theatre Royal[133] during the 'School for Scandal' of the Haymarket Company. During the 'screen scene' I was talking through the window to Madge Robertson[134] (Mrs Kendal Grimston) who did Lady Teazle.[135] At first I was nervous lest she*

---

133  The Theatre Royal, which opened in 1821, was located on Hawkins St., now the site of Screen Cinema.

134  Madge Robertson (1848–1935) was an English actress who married W. H. Grimston (stage name Kendal). Her popularity rivalled that of Ellen Terry.

135  Lady Teazle is a character in Sheridan's *School for Scandal*.

*might miss the cue for throwing down the screen but she laughed at my fears & they were soon forgotten. Bye and bye Joseph (Howe Hutchinson)*[136] *rushed over, put his head behind the screen & said most earnestly & persuasively – 'Keep close.' I rushed back fearing that something awful had taken place that the audience had heard our talking & laughter but Mrs Kendal laughed exceedingly as she reminded me that it was part of the play.*

7<sup>th</sup> of August, 1872

*Theatre Royal, Dublin*

---

136   Henry Howe Hutchinson used the stage name Henry Howe. He was a member of Irving's company.

→══ 224 ══←

*Dreamed last night about a mad female dramatic critic who got into a butter cask on board ship to shoot pirates through the bung-hole with a cross-bow.*

27th of October, 1871

→══ 225 ══←

*At one of the University Boat Club[137] Dramatic Performances at Ringsend the proceedings terminated with an impromptu dance. In the dance a lady and gentleman fell & there was of course a rush of all the men near to help the lady to rise. One horsey individual sweeping round in the valse called out instinctively, 'Sit on her head'![138]*

2nd of April, 1874

---

137 The University Boat Club, for which Bram rowed, was founded in 1836, rowing near where the Dodder flowed into the Liffey. In 1866, the club split into the Dublin University Rowing Club and the Dublin University Boat Club, but they were reunited in 1898 as the Dublin University Boat Club.

138 If a horse is injured, sitting on its head renders it immobile, preventing further flailing about.

### ⇒ 226 ⇐

*There is something of recollection in the pleasure of a 'grown-up' at a pantomime. Novelty is the child's delight.*

### ⇒ 227 ⇐

*J. A. Scott[139] told me he was once at the opera Theatre Royal. It was in the days when soldiers wore their uniforms off as well as on duty. In the dress circle front row was an exceedingly fat artillery officer who at the end of the first act stood up turned round and leaned on the back of his seat to talk to a girl in the row behind him.*

*A voice came down from the top gallery – 'Mr artillery officer'.*

*He of course did not hear nor heed – but many eyes in the house were turned towards him – a smile went round at his short tunic & massive proportions.*

*Again the voice was heard. 'Mr artillery officer'.*

---

139    Born in Dublin in 1854, John Alfred Scott became a member of the College of Physicians where he served as Examiner in Physiology and Histology. His son James was editor of the *Irish Times* from 1877–1899.

*Still he did not hear but the attention of the house became riveted on him & the audience waited.*

*Again the voice was heard – this time in accents of indignant reproach. 'Mr artillery officer – ah Mr artillery officer, will ye be plazed to turn the muzzle of your gun the other way.'*

*A roar which shook the house.*

⊷ 228 ⊶

*A man in the pit of the Theatre Royal thought he saw a friend several rows in front of him & wishing to attract his attention asked the stranger who sat immediately before him who had a stick to be kind enough to reach forward & poke his friend in the back, pointing him out for the purpose. The obliging stranger did so.*

*Immediately the pokee turned, the expectant friend saw the face of an utter stranger indignant with the unexpected aggression. Pokee asked poker what the devil he meant by his impertinent assault. Poker smilingly pointed to his neighbour who was regarding the curtain persistently with a stolid look on his face which indifference he persisted in maintaining. Thus poker taken red-handed was made a fool of & abused for being obliging.*

## ⇢⇥ 229 ⇤⇠

*T. Woodhouse told me he once went into a dingy theatre in a back street in Wexford. The place was lit by tallow candles & he & two friends were the only persons in the boxes. The play was Rob Roy, Helen being far gone in the way. All was so funny that the party could not help laughing so much that Rob Roy came down to the footlights and asked them what they were laughing at and ended by asking them (seriously) if they would like any other play better for that in such case he would be proud & happy to produce it instantly.*

## ⇢⇥ 230 ⇤⇠

*I once saw in the Queen's Theatre a cork thrown into the orchestra by some wag in the gallery. The launcher [Barrowcliff][140] who was very drunk stood up, stopped the band & made an oration in which he called the audience in the gallery assassins. He said, holding up the cork, 'It was only an accident & none of your fault that there was not a bottle at the end of it.'*

---

140   'Barrowcliff' is inserted into the text by Stoker.

*In 1852 Frank Seymour took the Theatre at Cork, got together as large and good a company as he could afford & went in for a big histrionic campaign. He was violently opposed by the parish priest who objected to the theatre in toto and who preached against the Company & undertaking & denounced them from the pulpit. The people were of course afraid to go and Frank saw blue ruin for himself & a 'dry up' for the Company staring him in the face. He was desperate & decided on a desperate game. He went to the priest & interviewed him. His reverence would at first listen to nothing; however after a while Frank got complaining to him that if he did not withdraw his ban, over fifty people would be thrown out of employment etc and asked the priest what he objected to. His reverence said, 'To the whole thing'.*

*'Were you ever in a theatre?' said Frank.*

*'I was not.'*

*'Then your reverence, isn't it very hard to ruin a lot of people for a thing you don't know anything about? Is it good or Christian? Will you come to the theatre and see for yourself and if there is anything you don't like I shall have it removed or stop playing altogether if you wish.'*

'But how could I go and with any presence countenance a proceeding to which I object?'

'Oh, that's all easy enough,' said Frank. 'Come behind the scenes & watch the play from the wings.'

His reverence considered for a while & then said, 'Well, I'll go just to satisfy my conscience but mind I shall oppose you all the same.'

The play that night was Macbeth. Frank gave instructions to his assistants to have everything they need & paper behind for his reverence and have special orders to the head carpenter to shift the front scene before the banquet scene at a certain signal & without delay.

The night came & the priest. Frank had sown orders <xxx> cart & papered the house from floor to ceiling. His reverence charmed & delighted with everything. Instead of drunken men he saw refined ones who talked in off moments on deep subjects. Instead of howling strumpets he saw demure girls who knelt for his blessing. The play wore on & whilst the banquet scene was setting Frank took his reverence in on the stage – long coat, shiny silk hat, umbrella & all. There was a stool in the centre of the stage. 'Won't you sit down your reverence,' said Frank and the priest sat on Banquo's stool. 'Fly Fleance Fly' was heard without. Just sit still a moment your reverence', said Frank. 'I'll be back in two skips of a dead salmon' and he left the stage, giving as he did so the signal to the carpenters.

The flats rolled back & on the astonished gaze of an immense audience burst the strange scene of their play-hating priest sitting on Banquo's stool.

There was a roar which shook the building. The priest rose, half maddened by the suddenness & strangeness of his position.

Down came the curtain as the priest rushed from the stage. Thence forward Frank Seymour had good audiences & in peace.

⤙ 232 ⤚

When [Irving] was playing Hamlet he was much troubled with a Horatio who would rant, & who in the scene where he tells Hamlet of having seen the ghost, would gesticulate wildly. Irving took him aside & showed him how he should speak & act the part. (Those who have seen & heard Irving read Horatio's part can understand the difference.) When he had done he said, 'Now my boy, you will do it that way tonight, won't you.'

'I will not sir.'

'And why not?'

*'Because sir, if I could do it like that I'd be getting my £80 a week as Hamlet.'*

### ⇢⇒ 233 ⇐⇠

*Henry Irving told me that he once gave a reading in a town in Scotland – Dunfermline.[141] (It was before he had played* The Bells.[142]*) He appeared on the platform & waited there a whole hour – but not one person came!*

[Marg: In 'The Stage Door' Christmas 1879]

### ⇢⇒ 234 ⇐⇠

*When we were in Belfast, Henry Irving, Loveday[143] & myself (H.I. went to give a reading for the Samaritan Hospital 16/8/78), we were at supper with David Cunningham. There were many speeches*

---

141   The town in Scotland where Irving was scheduled to read was Linlithgow, and the reading was to be 'The Lady of Lyons'. Irving wrote a humourous account of it in *The Stage Door* in 1879.

142   It was Irving's performance of Matthias in Lionel Lewis's melodrama *The Bells* in that brought him into the public spotlight. Starting in 1872, Irving would play the role 627 times.

143   H. J. Loveday would become stage manager at the Lyceum.

*giving Irving's health etc. One man said, 'Mr Irving, gentlemen, is known to you all. We know, gentlemen, whether others know that Mr Irving leads & has ever led a life of unbroken blemish.'*[144]

16<sup>th</sup> of August, 1878

→━ 235 ━←

*The same night after two men had each made two speeches re Irving, a third got up and said: 'Gentlemen & Mr Cunningham, Dr Mr David Cunningham our host, I would like to add a few words to those which have been so plaintively spoken by our friends here. I cannot sit by & listen unmoved to the noble praises of that worthy man – them unconscious gentlemen upright – upright as I said before – sir. I never sat at table with Mr Henry Irving before and I deem it to be the highest honour of my life. Yes, gentlemen & Mr David Cunningham our host, I swell with pride when I sit here at the table with Mr Henry Irving – the greatest genius of*

---

144 Stoker included this story in his *Personal Reminiscences of Henry Irving*, published thirty years later. Apparently he continued to keep his Journal at hand.

*his age – the greatest the world e'er saw. I feel as if I could sit here forever, gentlemen – and my old friend our host David Cunningham, Old Davy, than whom no man is more respected in Belfast no nor yet in Derry. And under the circumstances I hope you will let me go home. Remember, gentlemen & Mr Cunningham [this very plaintively] I have a wife & family. I have home duties to perform and I have to be at my office in the morning & so I will just say good night to you.'*

⊷⊱ 236 ⊰⊶

*Mrs A. Wigan was Miss Princott.*[145]

*Mrs R. M. moves in good society & talks of her family.*

*One afternoon some years ago, the stage manager of the Princess Theatre was coming away after rehearsal. At the door he was accosted by a labouring man.*

---

145 Actress Leonora Pincott (1805–1884) married Alfred Wigan in 1839 and was henceforth billed as Mrs A. Wigan. Her husband, as manager of the Queen's Theatre in London, formed a company that included Henry Irving. This story, from a much earlier time, was most likely related to Stoker by Irving during one of their Dublin meetings during the 1870s.

'I beg your pardon, sir. Are you the stage manager?'

'I am, my boy. What can I do for you?'

'Excusing the liberty, sir. But can you tell me if there is a Miss Princott in your theatre?'

'Princott! Princott! Let me see – yes, now I remember there is. She is playing a small part.'

'I hope she is doin' well, sir.'

'Oh yes, very well indeed. She is a good honest steady girl & respects herself & other people respect her.'

'God bless you, sir. Is she a good actress?'

'Well you see that's hard to answer. She's only doing a little at present but she will do more. She works hard & is well behaved & that's everything.'

'God bless you sir. Do you think she'll ever do much?'

'I should not be surprised – she is a good girl.'

'God bless you sir. I don't know how to thank you. You'll ex-cuse me sir for troublin' you when I tell you that I'm her bloody old father.'

On the American railroads it is not necessary to [get?]
your ticket before starting - as it can be got on board
Consequently some loafers make a practice of trying to [travel?]
free as far as they can When such are discovered the train
is stopped, specially on the Californian line, and the defaulter
kicked + put out on a morass or prairie if possible. On
occasion when the guard was collecting tickets after being
days out from California he came to a man who at first
pretended to be asleep & then said he had no ticket
The train was just then stopping at a station. The guard
asked for money: the passenger declared he had none
The guard accordingly kicked him severely a tergo +
put him out. Presently the train went on.

Next day, when the guard was again going his round
he saw the expelled one sitting calmly in his place.
he said "Did not I kick you out yesterday?" "I [guess]
you did" said the traveller. "how tell me said the [guard]
you have some game on. what is it? Do you mean to [travel?]
on this line without paying? How far do you are on to [go?]
"well" answered the traveller calmly "I mean to go to
New York — if my a--e holds out"!

# EIGHT

## ⇒ T R A V E L ⇐

Leaving their sons in Dublin in 1871 surrounded by a closely-knit network of Stoker relatives, Abraham and Charlotte along with Margaret and Matilda, then eighteen and twenty-five years old, prepared to depart for Switzerland. It was felt that Abraham's modest retirement pension would stretch further on the Continent. Over the next few years the four would live in Switzerland, France and Italy. This opened up for Bram the potential for travel to the Continent.

In 1874, he left Dublin for a short visit with his parents in Switzerland. But he never arrived. He stopped over in Paris and spent time with his theatre friend, Genevieve Ward, and was waylaid. Afterwards, he wrote to his father saying that he wanted to give up his job at Dublin Castle, move to London and write plays. Abraham Sr's admonition was swift: 'You know that there are few men of your standing now in the castle who have a larger income, and you can also guess how many competitors there would be if a vacancy took place tomorrow in your office' (qtd in Belford, p. 69). Bram would stay at Dublin Castle for another four years.

*Genevieve Ward*

In spite of his father's disapproval, Bram was not willing to give up his friendship with Genevieve Ward. Paul Murray draws attention to surviving correspondence between the two, noting the affectionate nature of their relationship; however, he hastens to add that 'it is uncertain if they were actually lovers' (p. 59).

Bram first encountered the American-born actress in November 1873 when he watched her performance as Adrienne in Legouve's *Adrienne Lecouvrier*. Captivated, he arranged an introduction. Years later in *Personal Reminiscences of Henry Irving*, he would write of this bond of friendship: 'There and then began a close friendship which has never faltered, which has been one of the delights of my life and which will I trust remain as warm as it is now till the death of either of us shall cut it short' (vol. 2, p. 169). They socialised together in Dublin intellectual circles, counting among their mutual friends Edward Dowden and Sir William and Lady Wilde.

Bram joined Genevieve in Paris again in 1875, this time returning to Dublin after a visit with his parents. He told them that he had decided to write a play based on an actress he had met, and rather than tell them the play was for Genevieve, he told them her name was Miss Henry. Abraham Sr was not amused. He wrote to Bram, stressing that in his lifetime he had known actors and actresses, and 'their society, while agreeable, was not desirable ... such acquaintanceship is better avoided' (qtd in Murray, p. 58). Bram continued to receive letters from both Genevieve and her mother, Lucy Ward, encouraging him to come to Paris and work on his play. The play, as far as is known, was never completed.

When Abraham Stoker Sr died in Naples on 12 October 1876 at the age of seventy-seven, appropriately it was Bram who travelled to Italy for the interment at the English Cemetery in Cava de' Tirreni. As he had taken on an active role helping to manage his parents' finances, his mother and sisters would have depended on Bram to help settle Abraham Sr's affairs. Circumstances would not allow the other four brothers to go to Italy. George had recently left Dublin to serve in the Russo–Turkish War; Tom and Richard were in India, Richard with his bride of one year; and Thornley's career responsibilities made it impossible for him to leave Dublin. When Bram returned to Dublin, Charlotte and her daughters remained in Italy; they would stay abroad for another few years.

Dating in the Journal indicates at least four trips to the Continent – 1874, 1875, 1876 and 1878. Scraps of detail from all four survive. They demonstrate two traits that we have already identified in Bram: his sense of incongruity and his keen eye for detail. Bram's appreciation of the incongruous is evident in his early impressions of Paris and Geneva. The 'ten thousand cocks … crowing all at once' is his imaginative way of reconstructing the harsh babble that emanated within the Paris Stock Exchange as traders communicated with each other (240). His imagination goes to work again as he finds a metaphor for Geneva: 'a big pigeon pie from the crooked chimney pots which look like the feet sticking out' (241).

Then we have his observations made on the train. Rather than comment on the landscape passing him by (as Jonathan Harker would later do in *Dracula*), Bram concentrates his eagle eye on the other passengers. He notes the nationalities and the physical appearances of those sharing his carriage en route from Paris to Geneva in 1875 (242). On another trip from Naples to Marseilles, he recounts a fascinating encounter with a Dominican friar who claimed to be an expert on curing the bites of scorpions and snakes (244).

Bram also had many opportunities for travel closer to home. Once he assumed duties as Inspector of Petty Sessions, between 1877 and 1878 he visited many communities around Ireland in order to monitor the duties of the other clerks within the system. This enabled him to see and experience the countryside, towns and culture throughout the country. He took advantage of it, duly recording interesting observations. He records entries from scattered locations: Counties Kerry, Mayo, Sligo and Monaghan; and towns such as Limerick, Wexford, Howth and Dundalk.

In the entry 'Authorship in a Country Inn' (252), we get a rare glimpse into the frustrations of an author who is trying to make headway with his writing while on the road. Apparently, Bram's Journal was never far from his side. Here he expresses exasperation about the intrusions, ranging from a snoring man in the corner to an argument between a patron and the waiter.

Once he took the position as manager of Irving's Lyceum Theatre (1878), his opportunities for travel increased even more: provincial tours with the Lyceum, occasional visits to the Continent for research and eight lengthy tours to North America. Remarkably, he never did visit Transylvania – except, of course, in his imagination.

## TRANSCRIPTIONS

### ⇥ 237 ⇤

*Exquisite love song. Aria di Salvator 'Star vicino al bel Idol che l'ama'.*[146]

**July, 1874**

---

146  The literal translation is 'Star next to the beautiful idol I have loved'. This piece of music (for voice and piano) is generally attributed to the Baroque painter, Salvador [Salvator] Rosa.

## ⊷≡◉ 238 ◉≡⊶

*'Le plaisir de mourir sans peine*
  *'Vaut bien la peine de vivre sans plaisir'*
  *Inscription of guest room in the Trappist Monastery*[147] *at Sept-Fonds*

## ⊷≡◉ 239 ◉≡⊶

*Cuban*[148] *singer (Miss Genevieve Ward)*[149]
*'Riki Riki Riki'*
  *'Quando sole de abano' or 'Polito' (chicken)*

---

147  This monastery is located in the Burgundy region of France, near the town of Autun. The inscription Stoker quotes is accurate. (Translation: 'The pleasure of dying without guilt is better than the punishment of living without pleasure.')

148  Born in the United States and baptised in Cuba, she later lost her voice after suffering from diphtheria in Cuba.

149  A singer as well as an actress, Ward remained friends with Stoker throughout his life. Stoker dedicated a full chapter to her in his *Personal Reminiscences of Henry Irving*. She was one of the small group who attended his funeral in 1912. In 1921 she was created a Dame of the Order of the British Empire, the first woman to be so honoured for services to the stage (Dalby & Hughes, p. 74).

### ⇢ 240 ⇠

*The first impression produced on a stranger going into the Paris Bourse[150] is that ten thousand cocks are crowing all at once.*

### ⇢ 241 ⇠

*Geneva is like a big pigeon pie from the crooked chimney pots which look like the feet sticking out.*

### ⇢ 242 ⇠

*Going from Paris to Geneva express there were in carriage. Self & English man. French lady & gentleman. Italian who lives in England with son (11) & daughter (16) pretty. Also an Italian (35) looked like Gennaro in Lucrezia.[151] He had bag of cigars & bottles of wine & brandy. Good fellowship all round. Effect of early morning sun. Gennaro*

---

150   The Paris Bourse was the Paris Stock Exchange. In Stoker's day, traders communicated on the floor through shouting and hand signals.
151   Gennaro is a character in the opera *Lucrezia* by Donizelli.

*looks old. French lady ditto. Young girl pale but beautiful – rest dirty.*

August, 1875

⸱ ⇢≡● 243 ●≡⇠⸱

*Travelling in the train from Foggia to Naples I was struck by the immense load the women carried on their heads, by the dust rising from the plough as the oxen dragged it through the earth.*

*A body of workmen came into the train. Each of them was equipped for travelling. Luggage of each consisted of a gridiron, a hatchet and a sack.*

16<sup>th</sup> of October, 1876

⇢≡● 244 ●≡⇠

*Coming from Naples to Marseilles by Niemen, Messagerie Maritime Company.*[152] *My fellow in cabin was frère Bernard au convent de Père Dominican from head of the order in Mossoul in*

---

152　The Compagnie des Messageries Maritimes de France. The *Niemen* was a steamship in its fleet.

*Mesopotamia.*[153] *Said he cured himself over 100 bites of scorpions thus. 'Get poison from one scorpion & put it in a phial, one fortieth part of this in a phial of water a fourth part to be drunk by the bitten person every two hours. Will make certain cure. The same rule does with snakes. Give poison internally.'*

⟶ 245[154] ⟵

*On the American railroads it is not necessary to get your ticket before starting as it can be got on board. Consequently some loafers make a practice of trying to travel free as far as they can. When such are discovered the train is stopped, especially on the California line, and the defaulter kicked & put out on a morass or prairie if possible. On one occasion when the guard was collecting tickets after being two days out from California, he came to a man who at first pretended to be asleep & then said he had no ticket. The train was just then stopping at a station. The guard asked for money: the*

---

153   The Dominican Order was established in Mosul (Mesopotamia, now northern Iraq) in 1750.

154   Stoker must have acquired this story second-hand, as his first trip to North America would not occur for several more years.

passenger declared he had none. The guard accordingly kicked him severely *a tergo* & put him out. Presently the train went on.

Next day when the guard was again doing his rounds, he saw the expelled one sitting calmly in his place. 'Hello', he said, 'didn't I kick you out yesterday?' 'I guess you did', said the traveller. 'Now tell me', said the guard, 'you have some game on. What is it? Do you mean to travel on this line without paying? How far do you mean to go?' 'Well', answered the traveller calmly, 'I mean to go on to New York – if my a—e holds out!'

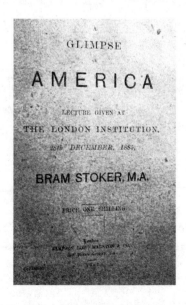

### ⟶ 246 ⟵

*A hatter met me in the streets of Naples. He was going about trying to sell one hat – the only one he had with him except that on his head.*

### ⟶ 247 ⟵

*In the 'black North'[155] I heard a girl say apropos of poverty, 'I'd liefer want better nor none at all.'*

*She also said apropos of a very ragged looking field: 'They labour the ground queerly in these parts: you'd think pegs was poking in it.'*

### ⟶ 248 ⟵

*Saw at Carrickmacross[156] two fawns fighting. They stood on their hind legs for fully ten minutes and appeared to almost hit out like boxers.*

---

155   Black North: Scotland. The name was given by the British following the Stuart uprising (most of the Stuart supporters were from the Highlands).

156   A town in Co. Monaghan, famous for its lace.

## ⤙ 249 ⤚

*In Co. Kerry I saw two pigs having a fierce fight and in Co. Mayo an angry battle between two geese.*

## ⤙ 250 ⤚

*The most unbusy place in Ireland is Collooney, Co. Sligo. There is no life at all at all. At the door of the police barrack there is a stuffed policeman – at least he looked such when I saw him. I fancied I could see all the bran stuffing running out of a crack in one of his boots.*

## ⤙ 251 ⤚

*An old woman in Co. Monaghan said apropos of poor Henry Wilson the oculist.*[157] *'An' shure sir, Pether went up to Dublin & was cured intirely in St Mark's hospital. An ye know acushla*[158] *it isn't*

---

157  The 'bastard' son of William Wilde, his surname was contrived as a contraction of 'Wilde's son'. A distinguished ophthalmic and aural surgeon, he died in 1877. One of his attending doctors during his last days was Bram's brother Thornley.

158  'Acushla' is a colloquialism for 'darling'.

*Saint Mark that has it now – but a cleverer man*
*be the name of Misther Docther Wilson.'*

⊷⊷● 252 ●⊷⊷

### 'Authorship in a Country Inn'

*I can't work. There is a colossal bagman sitting at the*
*table at the other end of the room. He sniffs perpetu-*
*ally & he sits on a chair which creaks as noisily as an*
*old ship in a storm at every word he writes. A peaceful*
*looking old man is snoring sterterously before the*
*fire. A tall traveller with an inflamed countenance*
*is having a 'go in' at the waiter about the fitness of*
*his chop. This latter old man is really too bad. He is*
*little better than a walking salad as he travels in*
*oil & vinegar. His tea drinking is a cyclone – his*
*eating is a storm – his sniffling is a hurricane. I*
*am waiting as patiently as I can for him to choke*
*– for choke he must & before long too if there be*
*any truth in scientific laws. Breakespeare*[159] *was*

---

159    Nicholas Breakspear (or Breakspeare) became Pope Adrian IV (1154-
       1159). He supposedly died from choking on a fly in his wine. Stoker
       was fond of weaving bits of historical information into his fiction. One
       need think only of the pieces of unrelated history that make up his
       background for Count Dracula.

choked by a fly. History they say repeats itself. I doubt it – at least it never repeats itself when you want it to – some people have great luck.

⟶ 253 ⟵

Madame Erenstein was giving readings from Shakespeare in Limerick. A countryman came up with his shilling in his hand & said to the doorkeeper, 'Whisper me now. Is there to be any tumblin'?'

⟶ 254 ⟵

I heard a peasant in Sligo say speaking of one of the political parties. 'They do go round an' round an' round an' round, jist for all the world like a dog lookin' for the head of his bed.'

⟶ 255 ⟵

'Rosey McCarthy's Quarrel with Mrs Reilly'

The people in Wexford was mighty bad intirely an' wasn't mindin' their offices at all at all – an' the priests was much concerned about them but they could do nothin'. So they axed the bishop

*& shure he sint down the mission fathers from Dublin – the up-late Pethers I think they call them. Well when the mission kem, the people gev over their bad ways an' all saved their souls, all but two women of the town be the name of Mrs Reilly an' Rosey McCarthy. An' these two women would not give in but laughed at the people to their faces.*

*They weren't in a good kind. Mrs Reilly was a bad woman – a real bad one, an' Rosey McCarthy wasn't what you'd call very good – she was the mother in hoors an' robbers, an' she was the daughter in hoors an' robbers, an' she was the gran-daughter in hoors an' robbers.*

*Well these two women held out till the day before the mission ended when lo an' behold good Rosey McCarthy gev in & went to Confession.*

*Mrs Reilly was very mad with her. She said that it wasn't fair iv Rosey – not for her to desart her like that an' she swore she'd be even wid her yet. An' so the people was expectin' that when the two meet there would be some fun.*

*An' shure enough on the Monday mornin' the women was washin' thar clothes down be the bed in the river. An' Mrs Reilly was there but Rosey wasn't.*

*An' presently they seen Rosey McCarthy comin' down the beach wid her clothes on her head. An' when Mrs Reilly seen her sez she, 'Girls', sez she, 'Here's Rosey McCarthy – look out for fireworks when she comes.'*

*Down kem Rosey McCarthy an' took down her clothes an' began beathin'. She took no notice of any one let alone Mrs Reilly. Mrs Reilly sez, 'Girls, here's Rosey McCarthy – the Bale o' Grace.' Rosey never minded. Mrs Reilly didn't like that so she ups & at her – she sez again,*

*'Oh girls, here's Rosey McCarthy. Ould Rosey McCarthy the suckin' angel an' if you'd rise up her dirthy ould shimmy ye'd see the down of her wings sproutin' out of her dirty ould shouldhers – so ye would.'*

*Rosey McCarthy never minded her no more awr if she was muck. Mrs Reilly got furious & she ups & ats her again & she sez with her face all red – 'Ould Rosey McCarthy, the bloody ould hoor – what killed more men nor ever Boney*[160] *done – no nor had whisky,' she sez.*

*Well, Rosey McCarthy couldn't stand that you know – so she ups too & she smacks her hands*

---

160  Napoleon Bonaparte.

*together & sez she, 'Mrs Reilly', sez she, 'Ma'am', sez she, 'I amn't goin' to bemean meself talkin' to you,' sez she, 'no nor to the likes of you', sez she, 'because I'm in grace so I am', sez she, 'an' you couldn't be', sez she, 'ye bloody ould bitch', sez she. 'I'm in grace so I am. But plase God I'll not be always so, an' if ye dare to say them words to me, you be the Hokey Fly',[161] sez she, 'but I'll pull the thripes[162] out iv ye.'*

⊰ 256 ⊱

*The old beggarman at Howth was being chaffed by an Englishman. He was proving for his English interlocutor that the Irish had done everything. The Sessenach[163] asked, 'An where did the Henglish come from?'*

*    'From England of course.'*

*    'Didn't they come from the Devil.'*

---

161    Well known Irish expression 'by the hokey [holy] man' – a mild oath.
162    Entrails.
163    'Sassenach' is Scottish for an Englishman.

*I drove from Crossmaglen*[164] *to Dundalk late in the afternoon October 77. The sun was without colour or light – all light was neutral. Away over south was a wide prospect of soft undulating hill & dale. There was colour all round, when one was close enough to see it. The blue-green of the turnip fields, the scarlet of the haws, the emerald of the flags & rushes. From the bogs rose a thick white mist that gathered & flowed away in the breeze like smoke. In the mist the turf stacks rose like islands. The clouds were heavy & neutral in tint. Together the sun & moon both pale & colourless & lifeless looked on the scene as though not participators.*

*Then the evening came quickly & the gleams of daylight faded. The moon grew mellow & bright. The mist drove in from the sea & filled the air. As we drove along the overhung roads, the moon-beams fell through the branches & slid down the lines of mist till every tree looked like a traceried window & the roadway was an ancient cathedral with the eternal moonlight following through the storied windows.*

---

164  Crossmaglen is in what is now Northern Ireland, just over the border.

*Bernard Lane[165] was telling in a hotel in Cork the following story told him by a man who was in the police court.*

*A street preacher had collected a crowd & refused to move on when ordered by the police. He was arrested & brought before the magistrate, Mr Flowers. Mr Flowers, not wishing to punish him but merely to prevent a recurrence, told him that he must find some friend to go security for his future good behaviour and said, 'Have you any friend?'*

*The preacher answered, holding up his hand, 'The Lord is my friend.'*

*'Oh yes, of course I know he is the friend of us all but have you no friend in London?'*

*'The Lord is everywhere.'*

*'Oh yes, I know', said Mr Flowers, 'but for the business purposes of the Court some person is required with a more definite residence.'*

*When the story was finished a man standing by said, 'That man's God was Baal,[166] I suppose.'*

---

165    Bernard Lane, an Irish tenor, performed in both the UK and Ireland.
166    In the Judeo-Christian tradition, a false god or demon.

⇢⇒ 259 ⇐⇠

*In Ballymote (Co. Sligo) 1877, I heard an angry man outside the hotel say, 'The nagurs, the nagurs, the dhirty nagurs.*[167] *They wouldn't give ye no not so much as a biled nail for yer coffin.'*

⇢⇒ 260 ⇐⇠

*On night of 17 June 1878 came to London from Paris. One of the men in the carriage with me was giving his impressions of Paris from which he was returning after his first visit. Some friend had taken him to the Jardin Mabille*[168] *on the Sunday night after the Grand Prix. He was a good lad & was horrified. Said he, 'It passed all I ever saw or heard or thought of. I wonder the Almighty did not rain down fire & brimstone on it – or I wonder what he keeps those articles for.'*

---

167  'nagurs' is clearly a rendering of the pejorative term 'niggers'. Stoker also uses the term in *The Snake's Pass* (p. 168).

168  The Jardin Mabille, known for its party atmosphere, had a famous outdoor dance pavilion.

# MABILLE'S FADED GLORY.

### *A CONTRAST WITH TEN YEARS AGO.*

### NO MORE GORGEOUS DRESSES AND JEWELS —A SICKLY SHOW OF PAID DANCERS AND HANGERS-ON—NOT EVEN ATTRACTIVE VICE—MOCKERY AND DELUSION.

*G. A. Sala's Paris Letter in the London Telegrap'*

I was at the Jardin Mabille in August, 186?. The crowd was as dense as that which thronged the gardens last Thursday, but what a difference

*Lough Gill Co. Sligo. Doonee rock at the end near to Sligo Town. Ben–Bulben is the mountain near.[169] A man of Sligo (McDonagh) once drew a bill in London as 'Ben Bulben Sligo' and cashed it with a money lender.*

---

169   Lough Gill is a freshwater lake situated mainly in Co. Sligo. It contains several islands, among which is the Isle of Innisfree. Dooney Rock offers a viewing point for the lake, while Ben Bulben is a large rock formation. The area features prominently in the poetry of W. B. Yeats.

"Putting two and two together"

There is a simple arithmetical calculation which is of vast importance – and yet one which is the cause of more evil socially and morally than calculators would believe – It is the putting two and two together. All scandals whether false or true arise from this – and it is a latent fact that true scandals form only a not-large percentage of the entire number. For the human nature is frail, human judgment is frailer still; and scandals arise – not because parties are guilty, but because strange conjunctures of circumstance occur.

night of. 15.9.71  1½ P.M.

# NINE

# ⊸⧉ OBSERVATIONS ⧉⊷
# AND MUSINGS

The entries in the Journal cover a myriad of subjects and themes, a manifestation of the range of Bram Stoker's interests and the fertility of his imagination. Though many of the notes gathered into this chapter are of the 'miscella-neous' variety, several offer a window through which we can catch a glimpse (albeit at times fleeting) of the man's outlook on life, his religious convictions and moral values, and even his political leanings.

The Journal reveals much about Bram's values as a human being and the way he perceived others. Having grown up in a family in which strength of character was endued by nature and nurture, his own morals reflected the values of his parents. Bram's father Abraham was by all accounts a gentle and righteous man. In a letter to his son in 1872, he wrote: 'Ever since I have had a family, a part of my nightly prayer has been that I might be able to rear them in honesty and uprightness' (qtd in Murray, p. 18).

*Arms of Stoker of Dublin, carried by the descendants of William Stoker (Bram's grandfather)*

Building on their seventeenth- and eighteenth-century trade guild associations, Stoker family members established themselves in the lower-middle-class bureaucracy, opening the way for successive generations to enter their chosen professions as gentlemen. Bram's grandfather, William C. Stoker, was a member of the Tailor's Guild of St John's in Dublin, and was granted the 'Freedom' of Dublin in 1780 by virtue of his apprenticeship as a stay-maker (corset-maker). Traditionally, 'Freedom' was ceremoniously awarded as a small parchment scroll in an engraved box of silver, gold or bronze, a milestone in the life of each young Irish man who worked to acquire it, and the right to vote that it conveyed.

There were at the time two classes of Free Brethren in Dublin: those admitted by birth, marriage or servitude; and those admitted by Grace Especial, a process by which if an individual was approved, payment precluded service. A Freeman's sons and grandsons were free by birth, and marriage to a Freeman's daughter might aid in the application for Grace Especial. However, in Ireland, very few Roman Catholics were granted the Freedom by Grace Especial, no matter how respectable the man or his profession. To earn his Freedom, an apprentice served five to seven years under a member of one of twenty-five Tradesman's Guilds, which regulated skills and trades from goldsmiths, butchers, bakers, bricklayers, brewers, to barbers and surgeons (the latter two being in the same Guild). In the case of the Tailor's Guild, the charter prohibited any non-member from making clothes in Dublin, and provided for the impoundment of such garments.

As he was a Freeman, William C. Stoker's sons and grandsons were Free by birth. A record from 1825 lists A. Stoker of Dublin admitted in 1822 by his birthright as Member of the Guild. Abraham, like his father and many others, maintained Guild membership although they were no longer, or had never been, involved in the trade. Abraham Stoker, who began working in Dublin Castle in 1815, was not trained as a tailor, but was elected an officer of the Guild, serving as Warden for one term, responsible for accounts and records.

Valuing the advantages of Guild membership as a framework for social life and future business and government connections, Bram Stoker later sought membership for his son, Noel, in one of the City of London's Livery Companies, or trade associations. With no birthright as a Freeman in London, Noel was apprenticed before the age of twelve, to gain his admittance to the Worshipful Company of Skinners. The Skinners, established in the 1300s, were originally engaged in the very profitable trading of furs and skins, and with their accumulated wealth, gradually evolved into an educational and charitable institution. Bram's great-grandsons have continued the family tradition of membership in the Skinners.

Bram Stoker lived according to his father's strong work ethic, paying homage to the Stoker family motto, 'What is true and honourable'. He would later take care to instil the values of his parents in his son, Noel.

Bram's mother, Charlotte Thornley, descended from the Blakes of Ardfry (County Galway), a large family with many branches. Their numerous landholdings and large estates, gained originally in 1681 by a grant of 12,000 acres, would ebb and flow through the years, through settlements, marriages and inheritances. In 1855, Abraham and Charlotte Stoker would benefit from the sale of Charlotte's inheritance, a share in 200 acres in County Mayo.

Growing up in Sligo in the northwest of Ireland, Charlotte had a childhood dominated by the horrors of the cholera epidemic of 1832. She was twenty-five in 1844 when she married Abraham Stoker, then forty-four years old and well established as a clerk. Charlotte was an intelligent and strong-willed woman who exemplified the ideals she instilled in her children. A short pamphlet she wrote entitled 'Rules for Domestic Happiness' (found among the family papers) clearly indicates her values of moderation and decency. Long before it was fashionable, but with the courage of her convictions, she advocated women's rights, specifically fair labour laws and working conditions. Education, achievement and success were expected in the Stoker household, and Charlotte guided her brood towards military and medical careers as a way to establish themselves in Irish society. As proper young ladies, the Stoker daughters were schooled in the fine arts. Though their parents were solidly middle class, each of the Stoker siblings would be well travelled, as well as respected professionally and socially.

Bram's moral compass is perhaps best shown forth in this statement about faith: 'It is very easy to have faith when your wishes are fulfilled. It is when your hopes are disappointed that your faith is tried' (285). That he had a religious upbringing is beyond doubt. The family had a strong relationship with the Church of Ireland (Protestant) in Clontarf and its clergyman, Edmund Nugent, who baptised each of the children. Bram's teacher, Bective Schoolmaster Rev. Woods, offered a strong religious component as part of their educational programme. We can assume that the family had a steady set of values based on Christian tradition, as would have been the norm at the time. Bram obviously perused his personal Bible frequently, as is indicated by the number of passages that are underlined. His great-grandson, Noel Dobbs (who now has the Bible) comments that these quotations give 'a good guideline as to how a man should live his life'.

His Christian faith is evident in several of his literary works. *The Primrose Path*, a story of drunken tragedy, contains much moralising, while a few of the stories in *Under the Sunset* have strong religious under-pinnings. As for *Dracula*, several scholars have noted the centrality of Christian beliefs in the novel. It can be viewed as a 'morality tale' that affirms the Christian premise that faith and prayer can overcome the power of Satan. Biblical phrases resonate through the text. Not only is Count Dracula associated with the Devil and repelled by holy symbols, he is also an inverted image of Christ whose arrival is heralded by Renfield, his insane 'John the Baptist'. Dracula offers the gift of immortality through the drinking of blood. A case can be made that *Dracula* is a reaffirmation of Christian teachings in the face of nineteenth-century scepticism.

In most cases, Bram's own values colour his perspective: the evils of spreading scandal (262), his advice for meeting challenges (265), his admonition concerning tolerance (278), his empathy (280) and the fine line between selfish and unselfish behaviour (282). He even includes a prescription for anger management (298).

Bram's selflessness and courage manifested itself in 1882 (after he had moved to London) when at the risk of his own life, he jumped out of a ferry boat into the swirling tides of the Thames in an attempt to rescue a drowning soldier. Though he was unsuccessful in saving the man's life, the Royal Humane Society awarded him its Bronze medal for his effort. Decades later, his son, Noel, provided this account to biographer Harry Ludlam:

Some time before 1882, [the Stokers] moved to 26 [sic] Cheyne Walk, whence my Father used to journey to the Lyceum by Steamboat. On the Evening of Thursday, the

14th September of that year, an elderly Fellow-Passenger, bent on Suicide, jumped off the Boat. Ignoring the strong Tide, my Father, without hesitating a moment, threw off his Coat and leapt in after him. Five minutes later, the Body had been got on board again. As Life was not apparently extinct, my Father had the man brought to his own House, but no Efforts could resuscitate him. For this Act of conspicuous Bravery, he was awarded the bronze medal of the Royal Humane Society, not being eligible for the Silver Medal, as life had not been saved. Henry Irving's letter to my Father, on this occasion read 'Sunday. My dear Bram. Look out tomorrow morning. You'll find yourself immortalised in the "Telegraph", or I'm a Dutchman. It serves you right old man! H.I.' Unfortunately, the Recollection of a clammy Corpse in the Dining Room, made my mother take a Dislike to the House; and, in due course, they moved to 17 St Leonard's Terrace, Chelsea. This would be about 1884.

A couple of entries provide a rare glimpse into Bram's political views. He developed distinctly Liberal leanings and, after his move to London, gravitated towards supporters of Home Rule for Ireland, such as British Prime Minister William Gladstone (with whom he later corresponded about *Dracula*). John Moore provides this overview:

*Royal Humane Society Bronze Medal*

Bram Stoker was born into and grew up in an Ireland that had become increasingly assimilated to British identity as the nineteenth century progressed. All semblance of an independent state disappeared following the legislative union of 1801 and he would have witnessed the decline of Dublin in particular, the former second city in the empire – politically, economically, and socially. This decline was accelerated by the disastrous potato famine that destroyed much of the population and impacted on every vestige of Irish society. Much of this fallout is directly and indirectly reflected in his jottings, across a wide spectrum of society, which he evidently encountered. His Anglo-Irish Protestant upbringing and education would have provided a degree of insulation but he was never immune or isolated from the 'real world' as his many astute observations, which are recorded, attest.

The years 1879 and 1880 marked a great transition in Ireland. C. S. Parnell established himself as leader of the Irish Parliamentary Party in the London Parliament and laid the foundations for Irish Home Rule. He was however most careful to accept the idea that the two countries would be linked by the monarchy – i.e. Queen Victoria would be our Queen. Stoker bought into this policy and was a leading advocate of Home Rule throughout his life. Indeed, many years later he discussed this with Gladstone the British Prime Minister during their many encounters. Early gleanings of his Irish Nationalist leanings are partly evident in one or two specific sections of this document.

Bram did not always take his politics seriously, however, as indicated by the inclusion of the mildly satirical distinction between conservatives and liberals (304).

Arguably one of the oddest entries in the Journal is the reproduction of a series of letters between a doctor and a patient (307). As the correspondence is dated 1870, a year before Bram began his entries, it must have been transcribed into the Journal at a much later date. Possibly the source of these letters was one of his brothers – William Thornley, Richard or George – all three of whom were practising medical doctors. In fact, the interest may have stemmed from Dr William Stoker's petition in 1836 to the House of Commons, in which he complained of 'not having been adequately remunerated for his services in extending the usefulness of the medical profession, and sedulously administering to the relief of the sick poor of Ireland for more than half his life.' It is also possible that Bram came across the letters in his capacity as Inspector of Clerks of Petty Sessions in Dublin Castle, while researching court proceedings for his book *The Duties of Clerks of Petty Sessions in Ireland*. Whatever the origin, they generate a good story.

## TRANSCRIPTIONS

### ⇒ 262 ⇐

### *'Putting two and two together'*

*There is a simple arithmetical calculation which is of vast importance – and yet one which is the cause of more evil socially and morally than the calculators would believe. It is the putting two and two together. All scandals whether false or true arise from this, and it is a patent fact that the true scandals form only a not-large percentage of the entire number. For tho human nature is frail, human judgment is frailer still, and scandals arise not because parties are guilty but because strange conjunctures of circumstances occur.*

**Night of 15<sup>th</sup> of September, 1871, 1 ½ PM**[170]

═══ 263 ═══

*One of the signs of the direst poverty that an honest man can show is a mended 'Jerry' hat.*

**26<sup>th</sup> of January, 1873** [Marg: <xxx> stories]

═══ 264 ═══

*'What a pity it is a man can't turn himself off like gas.' Carlile's friend*

**12<sup>th</sup> of July, 1873**

═══ 265 ═══

*Difficulties are like ghosts or wild animals. Look them steadily in the face & advance and they will recede.*

---

170   Surely he intended to write AM.

⇥ 266 ⇤

*There is a class of persons who seem to think that a man can have no taste unless there is something wrong with his inside: that aesthetic feeling and emotional power and fine delicate taste are centred in a broken back or a diseased heart or an abnormal liver.*

2nd of April, 1874

⇥ 267 ⇤

*Duff's Funeral*
*Mem*
*Write poor Duff's funeral*[171]
*Hurry etc*

⇥ 268 ⇤

*Situation. H. B. P. sketching behind the Buckstone,*[172]
*Forest of Dean & at this side the stone, girl sings,*

---

171  A reference to the funeral of Harvey Duff, a villain in Boucicault's play *The Shaughraun* (1874), at the end of which Duff leaps off a cliff to his death. Maybe Bram was considering writing a spin-off.

172  The Buckstone in Gloucestershire is a rocking stone, 19 ft long and 13 ft across, said to have been used in Druid ceremonies.

*'When the dove'. He answers with 'ruddier than the cherry', asked to join etc.*[173]

At the hill top a wicket gate leads us beneath the shadow of a group of deodars. Immediately at our feet on the steep slope is the great logan called the Buckstone; formerly, but now, alas! no more, a rocking-stone.

Here some may think it no more safe to dogmatize than when within the church. We are not prepared with a flat denial of the theory, still perhaps held by some, that the Druids not only used, but even poised and perhaps shaped the Buckstone. But we may at least allow ourselves to think geologists on safer ground. This block of old red sandstone conglomerate, with the slab on which it rests, is, as usual, of varying durability. A soft stratum has in all probability worn away until the stone was poised on a point comparatively small.

━━ 269 ━━

*Spring does not give or convey any idea of anything coming after. We live in the present only. Autumn especially late autumn does.*

---

173   The quoted lines are from Handel's *Acis and Galatea*. It is possible that Bram attended a performance of this opera in London in the summer of 1874 and that the lyrics were still fresh in his memory. We know that he was an admirer of Handel's work and would attend the Handel Festival (London) in 1877. Incidentally, Handel directed the world premiere of *The Messiah* in Dublin in April 1742.

⇥ 270 ⇤

*Furrows in the brow are chain marks or galls of an imprisoned soul.*[174]

⇥ 271 ⇤

*Some persons would judge character fairly but from the fact that they always judge by some one person or standard. Where the standard is limited, identity is wanting & the result weak.*

⇥ 272 ⇤

*'Fishing would be a good amusement enough if you were sure of catching nothing.' George Fitzgerald*[175]

---

174   This is yet another indication of the interest Bram had in physiognomy and its sister pseudo-science, phrenology. Popular during the nineteenth century, both attracted the attention of many writers, including Edgar Allan Poe, Walt Whitman and Mark Twain.

175   He was the brother of William Fitzgerald, who would illustrate (along with W. V. Cockburn) Bram Stoker's collection of children's stories *Under the Sunset* (1881). William is also believed to have drawn the five unsigned illustrations in Bram's serial novel *The Primrose Path* (1875).

*Sketch of Bram fishing (artist unknown)*

⭑⭑ 273 ⭑⭑

*A sporting man offered to back 10 to 1 a man he knew for a place in Heaven.*

⭑⭑ 274 ⭑⭑

*'What will you do when you are turned out of your office, before you go to Hell?'*[176]

---

176   One wonders who said this and to whom!

⤙ 275 ⤚

*Sectarian Education – 'Primary Secondary &*
*Tertiary'*[177]

⤙ 276 ⤚

*There are days in the life of each person of different*
*tone. Grey days – red days – dark days – bright*
*days etc.*

⤙ 277 ⤚

*J. B. Story*[178] *'How sufficient earnestness of purpose*
*in the general scheme of his life to make the absence*
*of it in detail noticeable.'*

A.S. 8th of November, 1874

---

177   Sectarian education was a source of much conflict between Catholics
      and Protestants, with both groups vying for the souls of Irish children.
      Religion, politics and revisionist history were inextricably linked.

178   A TCD graduate, J. B. Story was senior surgeon of the St
      Mark's Ophthalmic Hospital and later served as President of the
      Ophthalmological Society of the United Kingdom.

### ⟿ 278 ⟾

*One should have the same love & tenderness & toleration of the unconscious vulgarity of a self made man as for the weakness or pain of a child.*

### ⟿ 279 ⟾

*Whilst you are fighting a lion a wasp may be very unpleasant.*

### ⟿ 280 ⟾

*Why should some persons who claim refinement as the insignia of their order and the differentia of their personal identity think that they have a monopoly of all that is fair and true and regard with either wonder or condescension the outcome of fair spirits among the poor. There is beauty in a sweet soul – and we may see it, be its flesh garment fed on pistachio nuts or on husks.*

⇢ 281 ⇠

*Try and get a belief for yourself: and when you get it freeze on to it and keep it to yourself or some other fellow will burst it up for you. J. R. H.*

⇢ 282 ⇠

*There is a certain selfish relief in acting in a way which we consider unselfish. We feel relieved from all further moral responsibility of the consequences of our acts. Take care always that in acting as you think unselfishly you are not simply trying to rid yourself of responsibility.*

⇢ 283 ⇠

*A female servant was being married to a very decent fine looking young tradesman. Her mistress who was present & who had taught her to write noticed that she put her mark instead of writing her name & when she asked her about it said: 'Oh I can write ma'am but poor Joe can't & sure I wouldn't put him to the blush on his weddin' day. I intend to teach him to write too & then we both can sign what we will.'*

## ⟢ 284 ⟣

*It is a curious thing that when a house has been uninhabited for some time you will always find a lot of soot in the centre of the floor and pellets of mortar lying about – and a brown mark upon the wall.*

## ⟢ 285 ⟣

*It is very easy to have faith when your wishes are fulfilled. It is when your hopes are disappointed that your faith is tried.*

## ⟢ 286 ⟣

*Married man rich to unmarried poor man: 'You don't know what it is to lose money – when you go home and sit by yourself all the evening & won't speak to your wife & go to bed early – if any of your children come & sit on your knee you tell them sternly to get down out of that & go & sit by themselves.'*

## ⇥ 287 ⇤

*Col Ward*[179] *said that 'Peabody's soul had more play on the point of a Cambric needle than a frog in Lake Superior.' Also – 'When a man comes to my time of life he would sell out cheap.'*

## ⇥ 288 ⇤

*Strange revelation of a murder in a dream. Carlow*[180] *– watch in haystack. 1832 6*[181]

## ⇥ 289 ⇤

*How is it the cooing of pigeons always sounds like a sustained reproach.*

## ⇥ 290 ⇤

*'He hardly understood or realised the quiet routine life of those who are contented with their lot.'*

---

179  Genevieve Ward's father was Colonel Samuel Ward.

180  A county in southeast Ireland.

181  Maybe June 1832?

## ⇝ 291 ⇜

*Expression for mean manner of living – 'to whip the cat'.*

## ⇝ 292 ⇜

*Dr O'Shaughessy (Limerick) said in conversation, 'Eccentric I may be and doubtless am; but I am not a fool.'*

## ⇝ 293 ⇜

*'Oh yer honer', said the old beggar man. 'Musha bit yer not goin' away with the curse of the town on ye – without givin' a copper to a poor dark man.'*

## ⇝ 294 ⇜

*The same man said that England would not take 'home rule'*[182] *so Britain would lose Ireland – 'Shure*

---

182 Home Rule for Ireland was a dominant political issue in Britain and Ireland during the late nineteenth and early twentieth centuries. Its essential principle was the creation of an Irish parliament that would work within the British government.

*the Queen wouldn't like to lose an arm from off iv her crown.'*

## ⇢⇉ 295 ⇇⇠

*Dean Dickenson[183] & Archdeacon Lee[184] were having a conversation. E. J. Hardy[185] (author of 'How to be Happy Though Married') was present. Dickenson said, 'I would have the young ones brought up to a fixed rule – I would teach them nothing but dogmatic, systematic theology.'*

*'And', said Hardy afterwards, 'it sounded very cruel.'*

## ⇢⇉ 296 ⇇⇠

*Morris, The Chief Justice of the Common Pleas, said to Moffett, the President of the Queen's College Galway – 1877: 'Men seem to have lost the respect they used to have. I know that when I was*

---

183   Dickenson was Dean of Chapel Royal, Dublin. A strong supporter of temperance, he was widely known for his wit and congeniality.

184   Archdeacon Lee was a lecturer in Theology at TCD. He was one of a group of scholars assigned the task of revising the New Testament.

185   E. J. Hardy also wrote *Book on Manners, How to be Happy Though Civil* and *The Religious East; The Unvarying East.*

*a junior barrister, if a Judge looked at me I got a pain in my head – but now everything is changed. Everything & every person is challenged, from God Almighty down to the Chief Justice.*[186]

### 297

*One old woman who was very angry with some third person said in the street to another: 'Well Biddy, we may live in a cellar but for all that we aren't goin' to be p___d on.'*

### 298

*A preacher said in his sermon on the value of keeping temper and not answering unkind words with unkind words etc. said, 'And moreover my brethren, when a man is angry with you and abuses you, if you only keep your temper and do not answer him back, in nine cases out of ten you will aggravate him far more than you would by abusing him.'*

---

186  Bram's interest in the law probably originated with his work at Petty Sessions. He did continue it further and in 1890 was called to the Bar in London. Though he never practised law, his familiarity with it is evident in *Dracula*. Not only is the romantic hero, Jonathan Harker, a solicitor, but legal issues play a role in the plot.

## ⟿ 299 ⟾

*In Ireland there is a custom before Lent for men to throw salt over the girls to keep them fresh till after Lent. It is called ?*[187]

## ⟿ 300 ⟾

*The Apostle of Culture may be thus symbolized: 'An Ego seated on the summit of the Ineffable, shielding himself from the sun of Righteousness with the umbrella of Self-conceit.'*

## ⟿ 301 ⟾

*Note:*
    *The misery of one who is wrecked on sand – more paltry than destruction on a rock.*

---

187  The question mark is Bram's. We are equally puzzled, not even knowing whether Bram's tongue was in his cheek.

⇢⇢ 302 ⇠⇠

Note:

The strange waste of Death all the world over. The time & money spent on acquiring personal accomplishments which die with us & leave no trace. And further – the indirect value of the same.

⇢⇢ 303 ⇠⇠

Definition of Expression: the aggregate of the potentialities and the outcome of the training, habits & influences.

6th of September, 1878

⇢⇢ 304 ⇠⇠

### 'Conservative & Liberal'

'You ask me my opinion what is the difference between a conservative & a liberal. You want to know me opinion an' ye'll have it. It's this. A conservative man is a man that grabs an' clutches all he can lay his han's on and throughs it in close unto his buzzum. An' a *liberal is a man what gives away what doesn't belong to him.' Co. Down farmer to Tom Lage.*

⟶ **305** ⟵

*'A Pill for Aesthetic bums'*[188]

*I love England.*[189] *It is the only country in the world where you can see the meat hanging in the shops & then eat it.*

BS[190]

⟶ **306** ⟵

*To remove iron spots from prints or books (Dr Fraser, Harcourt St. Dublin*[191]*)*

---

188  'Bums' is an educated guess. Maybe this was intended as a snide remark at the expense of those offended by hanging meat. The word 'bum' was at the time (as today) a colloquialism for the human posterior.

189  One of the few references to England in the Journal.

190  After the death of his father in 1876, Stoker used the name 'Bram' and the initials 'BS'.

191  This is most likely Dr William Fraser of 20 Harcourt St., a contemporary of Stoker's at TCD.

1. *Put print in flat bath of permanganate of potash Condy's[192] purple fluid to deep purple colour). Let it remain for a few minutes till the paper gets a dirty brown colour.*
2. *Take out and rinse in water.*
3. *Put in a bath of plain water and add solution of oxalic acid (half full of tumbler to 18 inch both half inch deep).*
4. *Whilst this is acting, add teaspoonful of sulphurous acid.*
5. *Steep for a quarter hour in two waters – and dry.*

17th of November, 1881

※— 307 —※

*Correspondence of a Dispensary Doctor[193] (Locum Tenens)[194]*

---

192   Permanganate of potash is known as 'Condy's crystals'.

193   Under the dispensary system set up in Ireland in 1851, any poor person resident in the district was entitled to free medicine and medical advice on presentation of a red ticket. The system was subject to much fraud as well as abuse by patients well able to pay the costs.

194   Dr Mason was a temporary replacement for Dr Baird.

*(1)*

*Brook Farm*
*21 June 1870*

*Dear sir:*

   *As you are acting for Dr Baird, will you drop in here when you have time as I want to consult you on the subject of a slight indisposition under which I am at present labouring.*

                              *Yours truly,*
     *To: Dr Mason*          *T. White*

*(2)*

*2 Neville St.*
*21 Sept.*

*Dear sir:*

   *I would be glad if you will settle with me soon for my attendance in June & July. I sent a bill in August & enclose duplicate.*

                              *Yours very truly,*
     *To: T White*           *L. Mason*

*(3)*

*2 Neville St.*
*21 Dec 1870*

*Dear sir:*

   *I will be glad of an answer to my letter of 21*ˢᵗ

*Sept. I was much disappointed at not hearing from you sooner. I trust that I may not have to make a further application for the sum (£20) due to me.*

Yours truly

*To: T. White Esq.*            *L. Mason*

*(4)*

Brook Farm<br>27 Dec.

*Mr White presents his compliments to Dr Mason and begs to return his very impertinent letter. When I employed you to attend him, he did so as you were a public officer and of course paid by the State, and he further begs therefore to state that I will not enter into a litery [sic] war with a miserable surgeon.*

*To Dr (?) Mason*

*(5)*

2 Neville St.<br>1 January 1871

*My dear sir:*

*I am extremely sorry that you think fit to cut short our acquaintance, though only of a professional nature, in the preemptory manner stated in your letter. Before, however, meeting your wishes I beg to set you right on a question of etiquette concerning the public & the medical profession. In future when you may wish to obtain medical attendance without being obliged to disburse pecuniary emolument therefore your proper course would be to obtain a red ticket from a Poor Law Inspector which would entitle you to gratuitous medical relief at your own residence.*

*I am dear sir*
*Faithfully yours,*
*To T. White Esq.*            *L. Mason*


*(6)*

*1 January*

*You are a liar.*
*To Dr Mason*            *T White*

### ⟜ 308 ⟞

*'A Tragedy at the Piano'*

*The girl was asked to sing Lament of Anne Bothwell*[195] *but broke down – own secret story.*

15th of July, 1877

### ⟜ 309 ⟞

*'The People'*

*'The people – who are the People? When we talk of them in such a general way, we cease in our minds to deal with living, thinking, feeling entities and regard only abstract forms of thought. If such be not the case, how unjust are we then and how unwise? We would ask too much from them. We would have them bear in patience all the personal hardships from which we fain would shield ourselves and our order – and yet we would have them at the*

---

195　'Lady Anne Bothwell's Lament', a Scottish ballad dating back to the sixteenth century, tells the poignant tale of a young lady who, together with her child, has been abandoned by her lover.

*same time exercise all the moral restraint which in the scheme of the world's harmonious working must somehow & somewhere be exercised. What past have they in whose traditions to find a help as we have – what present have they working ceaselessly whilst they see others who do not waste revelling in the sweet luxury of ease – what future is to them – what goal towards which to look. Revoir ferme. Do not close all doors of time to those who strive in patience. The past ye cannot bring back or recreate. The future ye can only guess at – the present ye can make sweet. Ye can at least help to clear away the thorns which in the long season of neglect have there flourished. Ye can banish hunger & the dread of hunger – and suchwise sweeten the lives whose cups have bitterness from the brim to the dregs.'*

3ʳᵈ of October, 1873, 4ᵗʰ of June, 1882[196]

⟿ 310 ⟾

*'climbing the endless heights of troubled sleep'*

---

196    The inclusion of two dates suggests that the entry was originally written in 1873 but not copied into the Journal until 1882.

regular in its metre bu
copy it as it stood —

Of ready manner, and of good address
A little forward and not much refined
A total want of useless bashfulness
And a serene complacency of mind

An easy temper, hard but to trouble
A common rein which nothing can cont.
In fact so great a worship for a fille
His creed might be ! buffoonery of soa

Not that creed trouble him indeed at a
The Athanasian ever with its curse
He thinks more of the races and the ba
And leaves creeds to his sisters and the

He's fond of races — not their gambling p
But likes to see the struggle & the strai
The quivering limbs and panting hear
He don't like contents of the train

Yet these are harder and their prize
But he don't like them — he don't see th
Why should he bother over books to hee
And spoil his training ? he that wou

"just win a foot race — hast to the apple
"Drink all the kisses smiled into that

# ⋗≡ C O D A ≡⋖

One of the knottiest problems we had to resolve in preparing this book was to determine how to handle the eight loose sheets of paper inserted into the back of the Journal. They are clearly not an integral part of it: each inserted sheet is either smaller in size, unlined or blue in colour. We have no way of knowing when these pages were inserted or by whom. Nor can we establish whether Stoker ever conceived of them as being part of his Journal or whether someone (presumably a family member) at some date put them there in order to 'keep things together'. The latter is the more likely scenario.

The relevant sheets (all without page numbers) are as follows:

1. poem entitled 'Acrostic';

2. thirty-two lines of poetry (obviously incomplete) by an unknown author;

3. four pages (on blue paper) comprising early drafts of the poem 'Mary (4)' (Journal Entry 44);

4. untitled poem about Bram as a student at Trinity College.

Items 2 and 3 have been excluded. We have included 'Acrostic' (see Journal Entry 53), as it was clearly written by Stoker. Composed just over a year before he began the Journal, it introduces an intriguing love mystery.

An even greater mystery is provided by the untitled poem from Bram's Trinity College days. Although this poem was not written by Bram (and is therefore clearly not a journal entry), it is about Bram – and worth inclusion here, along with transcription and analysis.

## A. TRANSCRIPTION

## III

[Marg: <Henry xxx> Abraham Stoker 1868]

[Marg: This appears to me very irregular in its metre but I copy it as it stood]

*Of ready manner and of good address*
*A little forward and not much refined*
*A total want of useless bashfulness*
*And a serene complacency of mind.*

*An easy temper, hard but to provoke*
*A course vein which nothing can control*
*In fact so great a worship for a joke*
*His creed might be 'buffoonery of soul'.*

*Not that creeds trouble him indeed at all*
*The Athenaeum case with its curse*
*He thinks more of the races and the ball*
*And leaves creeds to his sisters and their nurse.*

*He's fond of races and their gambling part*
*But likes to see the struggle and the strain*
*The quivering limbs and panting heart*
*He don't like contests of the brain.*

*Yet those are harder and their prizes more*
*But he don't like them – he don't see the way*
*Why should he bother over books to pore*
*And spoil his training? No that wouldn't pay.*

*Just win a foot-race – hark to the applause*

*Drink all the kisses smiled into that cup*
*Ain't that a triumph in a noble cause*
*My lame ole tutor you may now shut up.*

*'Don't tease me with your prophecies sublime*
*'Altho some other fellow win next year*
*'He'll never finish it in such good time*
*'They'll never give him such a hearty cheer.'*

*He's not a braggart – so at least he'll say*
*And talk of nothing but himself for weeks*
*But does it in that epic-poem way*
*Which speaks the hero while the hero speaks.*

*A manly fellow with at times some sense*
*And always genial in his own rough way*
*With nervous callowness about as dense*
*As London fog on a November day.*

*There's just a glimmer <xxx> very <xxx>*
*But one wins prizes, that is ridicule*
*While fond of turning others into farce*
*He don't like others to think him a fool.*

*And he will soar into the realms of song*
*And get impatient if perchance you smile*

*When comic caution grows absurdly strong*
*From things before you its affected style.*

*Some say he is not merely what he seems*
*But <xxx> with many a hidden finer good*
*Heart hoping hopes – brain dreaming dreams*
*Ambition artless in the blood.*

*That he has sympathy for others' love*
*And love for others' sympathy*
*With mind to flow and heart to prove*
*And a high purpose – It may be –*

## B. ANALYSIS

First of all, this is a poem about Bram, as evidenced by the frequent references to athletics (races, ball, quivering limbs, joys of winning) and the allusion to 'his sisters and their nurse'. The date 1868 indicates that it was written while he was still a student at Trinty College and an active participant in athletic activities.

The same person who copied the text also wrote the marginal note beginning 'This appears...' The handwriting is not Bram's. This marginal note was clearly not written by the poet, but by a second party who was likely transcribing it from a lost original. Maybe it was intended to be part of some series (which would explain the heading 'III'). The 'Abraham Stoker 1868' appears to be in Florence's hand and was no doubt added much later (she and Bram did not begin their relationship until 1878).

*Bram with other officers of the Historical Society*

Who wrote the poem? If, as we suspect, Florence's marginal note begins with 'Henry', the poet may have been Henry Latchford, one of Bram's friends at Trinity (Journal Entry 208). This theory is given further credence by the fact that Henry had a special interest in poetry. He was a member of the 'Phil' and in November 1868 he delivered an address entitled 'The Educational Value of the Study of Poetry'. Surviving accounts show that Bram was present. Furthermore, there is a reference to Henry Latchford in Horace Traubel's *With Walt Whitman in Camden*: apparently Latchford had written Whitman 'in a wittily-facetious vein' (vol. 5, p. 246).

*A typical foot race in College Park, Dublin*

Was this poem Latchford's wittily-facetious tribute to Bram? Maybe it was some sort of 'spin-off' done as a joke or a 'roast'. The poem was written during the height of Bram's athletic achievements at Trinity, at a time when he was the recipient of several awards and trophies. Considering himself a well-rounded man, Bram may have been concerned that his athletic success might cloud his appearance as a serious thinker and a potential writer. Stereotypically, athletes (then as now) are not taken seriously as intellectuals. Bram did, however, prove himself to be equally adept in both spheres, as indicated by his record as an orator, a debater and a writer. This dilemma may have amused his friends, and set him up as the object of good-natured humour.

## CONCLUSION:
## THE NOTABLE BRAM STOKER

The latest date that appears in the Journal is 4th of June, 1882 (Journal Entry 309). At that point Bram stopped making entries (the last thirty or so pages are blank). But that was not the extent of Bram's note taking. Not by a long shot.

For starters, he kept a diary. Although the whereabouts of the original are currently unknown, we know of its existence because Bram refers to it at least a dozen times in *Personal Reminiscences of Henry Irving*. The earliest reference is to an entry dated 29 November 1873, an indication that he was keeping it simultaneously with the Journal. This entry comprised a brief note about Genevieve Ward whom he had recently met at the theatre: 'Mem. Will be a great actress' (vol. 2, p. 169). On 14 February 1876, he wrote 'Spoke – I think well' of his participation in a debate on Walt Whitman's poetry at Trinity College (vol. 2, p. 96).

Having been approached by Henry Irving on 22 November 1877 about a possible position should he acquire his own theatre, Bram jotted 'London in view!' (vol. 1, p. 54). Other entries concern Irving, the Lyceum and various activities related to life and work at the theatre, including a lengthy record of a visit with Franz Liszt (vol. 2, p. 147) and a prophetic statement made after having met Theodore Roosevelt in 1895 that he 'must be President some day' (vol. 2, p. 236).

His son Noel, during interviews with Harry Ludlam in the late 1950s, emphasised his father's obsession with keeping records:

> When he wrote 'Henry Irving' in 1906, he was able to say how many times each Play had been performed; and the Total of their Earnings. The jotted Diary, which he kept, never failed him; and it is noticeable that he was never at a Loss for a Date. It is, I think, another sign of his Love and Devotion for his Friend [Irving] that, however long had been the Day – or Night, the Record in that Diary was never deferred. (Stoker Family Papers)

Of course, record keeping had been an essential part of his work with Petty Sessions at Dublin Castle. That experience was excellent preparation for his duties at the Lyceum Theatre where one of his main responsibilities was to keep the accounts. Collector John Moore has in his possession one of Stoker's ledger books from that period. This Ledger was actually a custom printed accounts book that Bram must have designed specifically for the tours. Each double page gave him room to keep track of all the pertinent receipts and costs for each engagement. It is obvious that he kept an eye on the proverbial 'bottom line', as the book is set up to record profits for each week and for the whole tour to date.

Then there are Stoker's notes for his most famous work, *Dracula*. Composed over a seven-year period from 1890 to 1896, the 124 pages comprising the *Dracula* notes are currently housed at the Rosenbach Museum & Library in Philadelphia. They provide a wealth of information about Stoker's research for the novel as well as his construction of plot and development of characters. They display many of the same traits found in the Dublin writings: a keen eye for detail and a passion for observing and recording. An essential resource for any serious researcher or scholar of Stoker/*Dracula*, the *Dracula* Notes have been published in a facsimile edition with commentary and annotations by Robert Eighteen-Bisang and Elizabeth Miller.

'I seldom wrote, in working times, less than fifty letters a day' (*Personal Reminiscences*, vol. 1, p. 42).

Bram Stoker left behind volumes of letters, notes and telegrams that now form parts of major collections in libraries and museums, notably the following: the Bram Stoker Theatre Collection, Shakespeare Centre Library, Stratford-upon-Avon; and the Brotherton Collection, University of Leeds. Family correspondence and other related papers are gathered in the Stoker Family Collection, Trinity College Dublin. The written record is indeed extensive.

# ⇒ WORKS CITED ⇐

Belford, Barbara. *Bram Stoker: A Biography of the Author of* Dracula. New York: Knopf, 1996.

Dalby, Richard and William Hughes. *Bram Stoker: A Bibliography*. Westcliff-on-Sea, UK: Desert Island Books, 2004.

Davies, Bernard. 'Inspirations, Imitations and In-Jokes in Stoker's *Dracula*', in Elizabeth Miller, ed. *Dracula: The Shade and the Shadow*. Westcliff-on-Sea, UK: Desert Island Books, 1998, pp. 131-7.

Eighteen-Bisang, Robert and Elizabeth Miller, eds. *Bram Stoker's Notes for* Dracula: *A Facsimile Edition*. Jefferson, NC: McFarland, 2008.

Farson, Daniel. *The Man Who Wrote* Dracula: *A Biography of Bram Stoker*. New York: St Martin's Press, 1975.

Gerard, Frances A. *Picturesque Dublin*. Hutchinson & Co., 1898.

Graves, C. L. 'The Lighter Side of Irish Life'. *Quarterly Review*, vol. 219, no. 436, pp. 26-47.

Holroyd, Michael. *A Strange Eventful History*. London: Vintage, 2009.

Leahy, M. P. 'Dublin University Boat Club Reminiscences', in Kenneth C. Bailey, *A History of Trinity College Dublin, 1892–1945*. Dublin: Hodges Figgis, 1947.

Leatherdale, Clive. *Dracula: The Novel & the Legend*. Third edition. Westcliff-on-Sea: Desert Island Books, 2001.

Ludlam, Harry. *My Quest for Bram Stoker*. Chicago: Adams Press, 2000.

Miller, Elizabeth. *Bram Stoker's* Dracula: *A Documentary Journey into Vampire Country and the Dracula Phenomenon*. New York: Pegasus Books, 2009.

Murray, Paul. *From the Shadow of* Dracula: *A Life of Bram Stoker*. London: Jonathan Cape, 2004.

*Reminiscences of Sir Charles Cameron, C. B*. Dublin: Hodges Figgis, 1913.

Stoker, Bram. 'Author's Preface', *Makt Myrkranna* [Icelandic edition of *Dracula*]. 1901. Repr. in Elizabeth Miller, *Bram Stoker's* Dracula: *A*

*Documentary Journey*. New York: Pegasus Books, 2009, pp. 278-9.

Stoker, Bram. *Dracula*. London: Constable, 1897.

Stoker, Bram. 'Mr Winston Churchill'. 1908. Repr. in Richard Dalby, ed. *A Glimpse of America and Other Lectures, Interviews and Essays*. Westcliff-on-Sea, UK: Desert Island Books, 2002, pp. 121-6.

Stoker, Bram. *Personal Reminiscences of Henry Irving*. 2 vols. London: Macmillan, 1906.

Stoker, Bram. *The Snake's Pass*. 1890. Chicago: Valancourt Books, 2006.

Stoker, Bram. *Snowbound: The Record of a Theatrical Touring Party*. 1908. Annotated and edited by Bruce Wightman. Westcliff-on-Sea, UK: Desert Island Books, 2000.

Stoker, Bram. *The Watter's Mou'*. New York: Theo De Vinne & Co., 1894.

Stoker Family Papers. Trinity College Dublin.

Terry, Ellen. *The Story of My Life*. London: Hutchinson & Co., 1908.

Traubel, Horace. *With Walt Whitman in Camden*. Vol. 5. Carbondale: Southern Illinois University Press, 1964.

Whitman, Walt. *Letter to Bram Stoker*. 6 March 1876. In Bram Stoker, *Personal Reminiscences*, vol. 2, p. 97.

# ⚍ PAGINATION KEY ⚍

Entry# (left-hand column) Stoker page# (right-hand column)

# ⇒ B R A M   S T O K E R ⇐
# & F A M I L Y   T I M E L I N E

[Authors' note: We have made every effort to provide accurate data based on existing biographies and documented records.]

<u>1799</u>
Abraham Stoker Sr is born in Dublin, youngest of six children of William Stoker and Frances Smyth. (12 March)

<u>1815</u>
Abraham Stoker, 16, enters Civil Service as a clerk in the Chief Secretary's Office, Dublin Castle. (June)

<u>1817</u>
Charlotte Matilda Blake marries Lt Thomas Thornley. (3 October)

<u>1818</u>
Charlotte Matilda Blake Thornley (Bram's mother) is born in Sligo. (28 June)

**1822**
Abraham Stoker Sr receives the Freedom of Dublin and the right to vote.

**1824**
Abraham Stoker Sr serves as Warden (accountant) of the Tailor's Guild for one year.

**1832**
Charlotte Thornley (Bram's mother), age 14, lives through the horrors of the cholera epidemic in Sligo.

**1833**
Abraham Stoker Sr is put in charge of parliamentary business in the Chief Secretary's Office at Dublin Castle.

**1836**
Although still listed as a Junior Clerk at Chief Secretary's Office, Abraham's title of Esquire denotes a status above that of 'gentleman'.

**1844**
Abraham Stoker Sr marries Charlotte Matilda Blake Thornley at Coleraine Parish Church, Co. Derry. (16 January)

**1845**
First child, William Thornley, is born. Ellen Crone, who remains with the family for years as the children's nurse, cares for him. (6 March)
    Potato blight arrives in Ireland, ruining half of the annual potato harvest. The Great Famine begins.
    The Stokers are living at 15 Marino Crescent, Clontarf, a suburb of Dublin.

**1846**
Charlotte Matilda Stoker is born at 15 Marino Crescent. (9 June)

## 1847
('Black 47')

Famine worsens after an exceptionally bad winter. Typhus epidemic kills tens of thousands in Ireland.

Abraham Stoker Jr is born at 15 Marino Crescent. (8 November)

Abraham Jr is baptised in Clontarf by Edmund Nugent, Church of Ireland priest. (30 December)

## 1848-49

Famine continues, along with outbreaks of cholera and repeated failure of potato harvest.

## 1849

Abraham and Charlotte Stoker's fourth child, Thomas, is born at Killester, outside Dublin. (20 August)

## 1850

The Great Famine ends.

## 1851

Richard Nugent Stoker, fifth child of Abraham and Charlotte Stoker, is born at Killester. (31 October)

Population of Ireland is 6,575,000 – a drop of 1,600,000 in ten years.

## 1853

Margaret Dalrymple Stoker, sixth child, is born at Artane Lodge, near Killester. (20 March)

After forty years at Dublin Castle, Abraham Stoker Sr, Esq. applies and is accepted for the position of Senior Clerk.

## 1854

George Stoker, the last of the Stokers' seven children, is born at Artane Lodge. (20 July)

Young Abraham 'Bram' Stoker, age 7, overcomes undiagnosed illness.

## 1858

Florence Ann Lemon Balcombe, future wife of Bram Stoker, is born in Falmouth, Cornwall, England, daughter of Lt Col James Balcombe. (17 July)

The Stoker family moves to 17 Upper Buckingham Street, nearer to Dublin city centre, in the Mountjoy area of N. Dublin.

Abraham 'Bram' Stoker attends Bective House College at 15 Rutland Square.

## 1861

Census shows population of Ireland as 5,800,000, a decrease of over 11 per cent since 1851.

Abraham (Bram) Stoker and his sister, Matilda, win prizes (of books and drawing materials) for drawing in the Royal Dublin Society's competitions.

## 1863

W. Thornley Stoker moves into 43 Harcourt St., Dublin.

Charlotte Stoker, an associate member, reads her paper on 'The Necessity of a State Provision for the Education of the Deaf & Dumb in Ireland' at a meeting of the Statistical & Social Inquiry Society. (13 May)

## 1864

Charlotte Stoker addresses the Statistical & Social Inquiry Society on 'The Situation with Female Emigration from Workhouses in Ireland'. (20 January)

Bram enters Trinity College Dublin just before his seventeenth birthday. Matilda Stoker receives honourable mention from Taylor Prizes, Dublin for Painting from Life, and the prize awarded by the Department of Science and Art for Freehand and Perspective.

## 1865

The City of Dublin Election Rolls lists Abraham Stoker, Esq. at 4 Orwell Park, Rathgar. (July)

Abraham C. Stoker, Esq. retires as 1st Class Clerk, after more than fifty years of service at Dublin Castle. (26 November)

## 1866

Abraham (Bram) Stoker, age 18, joins the Civil Service at Dublin Castle, while still a student at Trinity College Dublin. (9 April)

William Thornley Stoker receives his medical degree from Queens University, Galway, and begins private teaching.

## 1866-71

While a student at Trinity College Dublin, Bram Stoker receives awards and medals for walking races, foot races and weightlifting.

As a member of Trinity Rugby Club, Bram plays for 1st and 2nd XVs, receives caps, becomes member of the committee.

## 1868

Walt Whitman's *Leaves of Grass* is published in the British Isles.

## 1870

Abraham (Bram) Stoker reads 'Means of Improvement in Composition' at the Trinity College Philosophical Society.

Abraham (Bram) Stoker graduates from Trinity.

After an open testing competition, Tom Stoker is appointed to the Bengal Civil Service.

## 1871

Bram Stoker takes a position to defend Walt Whitman at a meeting of the Trinity College Philosophical Society. (May)

Bram Stoker begins entries in his journal. (August)

Bram Stoker begins writing theatre reviews in the *Dublin Evening Mail.* (November)

## 1872

Bram Stoker writes to Walt Whitman, but does not send letter until 1876. (18 February)

After two years training, Tom Stoker arrives in NW Provinces, India serving as assistant magistrate & collector with the Bengal Civil Service. (14 November)

Bram's parents and two sisters, Matilda and Margaret, depart for Switzerland.

Bram publishes his first story, 'The Crystal Cup'.

## 1873

Bram Stoker meets American-born actress Genevieve Ward in Dublin, beginning a lifelong friendship. (November)

Bram becomes the editor of the *Irish Echo*. (until 1874)

## 1873

Richard N. Stoker, living at 43 Harcourt St. with Thornley, is licensed by the Royal College of Surgeons.

## 1874

Bram Stoker is a founding member of The Dublin Sketching Club. (October)

Bram, waylaid en route to visit his family in Switzerland, visits Genevieve Ward in Paris.

Bram moves in with his brother, W. Thornley Stoker at 16 Harcourt St.

## 1875

Dr. W. Thornley Stoker marries Emily, age 25, daughter of William Stewart, at St Barnabas Church, Middlesex, England, witnessed by Abraham Stoker Jr. (August 3)

*The Primrose Path* is published.

Bram Stoker again visits Genevieve Ward in Paris.

## 1876

At age 77, Abraham C. Stoker, Esq. dies in Naples, Italy. Bram goes to Italy for the interment at the English Cemetery in Cava de' Tirreni. His mother and two sisters remain abroad. (12 October)

Bram Stoker meets Henry Irving following Bram's positive review of *Hamlet*. A close bond is formed between the two men. (29 November)

Bram organises a reception for Henry Irving in Dublin, including a 'College Night' at the theatre and a popular procession during which the students draw the actor's carriage through the city. (3 December)

Oscar Wilde meets Florence Balcombe.

George Stoker leaves Dublin to serve in the Russo–Turkish War.

Bram Stoker is promoted to Inspector of Petty Sessions, Dublin Castle.

### 1877

Bram Stoker moves to 7 St Stephens Green.

### 1878

Margaret Dalrymple Stoker marries a colleague of Thornley Stoker's, Dr. William Thomson, surgeon, who lives at 31 Harcourt St. (27 June)

Bram Stoker resigns his position at Dublin Castle. (late November)

The marriage of Florence Ann Lemon Balcombe and Bram Stoker takes place at St Ann's Church, Dawson St., Dublin. (4 December)

Bram leaves Dublin for London to work as manager of Irving's Lyceum Theatre. Bram and Florence Stoker move into 7 Southampton St., Covent Garden, London. (9 December)

Dr George Stoker publishes his war experiences in *With the 'Unspeakables', or Two Years Campaigning in European and Asiatic Turkey*.

### 1879

*Duties of Clerks of Petty Sessions in Ireland* by Bram Stoker is published, remaining in use as a manual until 1960s.

Genevieve Ward rents the Lyceum Theatre while Henry Irving is away on summer holiday. Bram Stoker counsels her on her selection of plays.

Irving Noel Thornley Stoker, son of Florence and Bram Stoker, is born at 7 Southampton St., London. (30 December)

1881

The London Census lists Bram Stoker, age 33, theatrical manager; Florence, age 21, artist; Noel, baby; George Stoker, age 26, physician & surgeon; servants: Harriet, 21, cook; Emma, 15, housemaid; & Elizabeth, 30, nurse living at 27 Cheyne Walk, Chelsea.

Bram Stoker's book of children's stories, *Under the Sunset*, is published.

1882

About 6 p.m., Bram Stoker risks his life, trying to save a man drowning in the Thames. For his efforts, he is awarded the Humane Society Medal. (14 September)

1883

Bram Stoker and Henry Irving undertake first of eight Lyceum Theatre tours in America.

1884

Bram visits Walt Whitman at his home in Camden, New Jersey. (20 March)

1885

Bram lectures at The London Institute on 'A Glimpse of America'. (28 December)

1886

Florence and Noel Stoker escape from the wreck of steamship *Victoria* crossing the English Channel, near Dieppe. (13 April)

Using Walt Whitman's 'Memoranda During the War' as his source, Bram Stoker lectures on Abraham Lincoln at Chickering Hall, New York. (25 November)

Bram Stoker's *A Glimpse of America* is published.

Charlotte Stoker returns to Dublin to live.

1888

Jack the Ripper murders prostitutes in Whitechapel, London.

## 1890

Bram begins first notes for what would become *Dracula* (March 8)

Bram Stoker is called to the English Bar. (30 April)

Bram spends three weeks at Whitby, staying at 6 Royal Crescent.

*The Snake's Pass*, Bram Stoker's novel set in Ireland, is published.

## 1891

George Stoker is living at 14 Hertford St., London with wife Agnes, two children, cook, parlour maid, housemaid, and governess (age 24) named Minna.

## 1894

Bram's novel, *The Watter's Mou'* is published.

## 1894-1895

W. Thornley Stoker serves as president of Royal College of Surgeons in Dublin.

## 1894-96

Bram spends summers in Cruden Bay, Scotland, working on *Dracula*.

## 1895

Portrait of Florence Stoker by Rathmines native, Walter Osborne, is exhibited at the Royal Academy in London. (Summer)

Bram's novel, *The Shoulder of Shasta*, is published.

Stoker is involved with Mark Twain in unsuccessful typesetting scheme of Paige Compositor Manufacturing Co. Project is overwhelmed by competitor Mergenthaler's Linotype.

Henry Irving and William Thornley Stoker are knighted by Queen Victoria.

## 1897

Dramatic reading of *Dracula* is held at Lyceum to protect copyright. (18 May)

1897
*Dracula* is published. (26 May)

Bram, Florence and Noel Stoker move to 18 St Leonard's Terrace, Chelsea, London.

1898
Fire destroys Lyceum scenery in storage. (18 February)

Bram's novel, *Miss Betty*, is published.

1899
*Dracula* first published in the US by Doubleday & McClure, New York.

Henry Irving falls ill with pleurisy, and without consulting Bram, signs away Lyceum to consortium.

1901
After living for fifteen years at 72 Rathgar Rd, Dublin, Charlotte Stoker, age 82, dies of cardiac arrest brought on by influenza, with interment at Mt Jerome Cemetery, Dublin. (15 March)

Canadian Census lists retired physician, Richard N. Stoker and wife, Susan, residing at Lake Cowichan, Vancouver Island, BC.

Census records for London list George Stoker, surgeon; wife, Agnes; children, Sheila and Tom; cousin, Bruce Metcalfe; and three Irish servants, at St George Hanover Square.

1902
Bram spends summer at The Crookit Lum (cottage) at Cruden Bay.

Bram's novel, *The Mystery of the Sea*, is published.

1903
*The Jewel of Seven Stars* is published.

**1905**
After performing his adaptation of Tennyson's *Becket*, Henry Irving collapses and dies at the Bradford Hotel. (13 October)
*The Man* is published.

**1906**
Bram Stoker's *Personal Reminiscences of Henry Irving* is published.

**1907**
Bram's health declines after Irving's death in 1905. He suffers a minor stroke, is nursed by Florence and they move to 4 Durham Place (former home of Captain Bligh of 'Mutiny on the Bounty' fame).

**1908**
Both Bram's collection of stories, *Snowbound: The Record of a Theatrical Touring Party* and his novel, *Lady Athlyne*, are published.

**1909**
*The Lady of the Shroud* is published.

**1910**
I. Noel T. Stoker (Bram's son) marries Neelie Moseley Deane Sweeting. (30 July)
   *Famous Impostors* is published.
   Bram suffers his second stroke.

**1911**
Bram, Florence and Noel move from Chelsea to 26 St George's Square, Belgravia (London)
   Bram appears as model for 'William II Building the Tower of London' in Goldsborough Anderson's mural in the Royal Exchange (London).
   Bram publishes his last novel, *The Lair of the White Worm*.

## 1912
Bram Stoker dies in London five days after the sinking of the *Titanic*. (20 April)
  William Thornley Stoker dies in Dublin. (1 June)

## 1913
Florence Stoker sells Bram's literary effects in Sotheby's auction. (7 July)

## 1914
Florence moves to 4 Kinnerton Studios (now Braddock Hse), Knightsbridge.
  Florence releases Bram's *Dracula's Guest and Other Weird Stories*.

## 1922
Prana Films releases *Nosferatu*. Florence starts *Dracula* copyright infringement case.

## 1925
Florence wins copyright case. Prana Films declares bankruptcy.

## 1927
Florence authorises the Deane and Balderston stage-play adaptation of *Dracula*.

## 1931
Universal Studios releases Tod Browning's movie, *Dracula*, starring Bela Lugosi as Count Dracula. (12 February)
  Richard Nugent Stoker, 79, dies at Duncan BC, Canada. (14 June)

## 1937
Florence Ann Lemon Balcombe Stoker dies in London. (25 May)

## 1961
Irving Noel Thornley Stoker dies at Bloomsbury (London).

# ⊷ AFTERWORD ⊶

The decision by my cousin, Noel Dobbs, to facilitate the publication of Bram's Journal in effect transforms this private, family treasure into a piece of literary history, and I thank him for allowing me to be part of that transformation. How appropriate that we are bringing this material to light in 2012, the centenary of Bram Stoker's death. The process has been enriching on so many levels, certainly humbling and at times overwhelming.

Noel has commented on his personal connection with a Journal entry made by his great-grandfather in 1874:

*Love can only be made in perfection beside the sea.* (151)

In addition to his literary legacy, Noel explains that Bram's direct descendants inherited Bram's passion for the sea:

On a day trip from London in 1927 our grandmother, Neelie (Noel's wife), bought four tiny, very run down cottages in a village on the Isle of Wight called Seaview (built in 1640). These were converted into two cottages – the first (Saltmeads) soon after the purchase and the second (Salterns) after the funds from the sale of the film rights to *Dracula* were received in 1932.

My brother Jamie and I were evacuated to our grandmother's on the Isle of Wight in 1942, and then spent the rest of the war years living happily here (note that our father was killed in a Royal Navy flying accident in May 1939 and our mother Ann was working in London during the war). Our grandparents in effect brought up Jamie and me. Living in Seaview we developed our love of the sea, encouraged by a slightly older friend whose father was a yachting correspondent and writer on marine matters. Our school holidays were always spent in Seaview where we sailed and raced continuously.

Jamie and I started working in London in the late 1950s and we came to Seaview in the summer almost every weekend and again for our holidays. In the early 1960s, Jamie 'went sailing' and eventually ended up in the West Indies and Bahamas, later buying a 41ft yacht on which he has effectively lived for the last thirty-five years. I continued to largely work in London, except for a two-year period spent in New Zealand where we cruised and raced for ten months of the year.

After Susan and I were married, we continued to come to Seaview on weekends and for holidays and our children knew little alternative! All three sailed and both our sons now have cruising yachts and their children are learning to sail. Susan spent some of the war years on St Michael's Mount, a small island off the Cornish coast owned by her mother's family, so the sea is in her blood as well.

Robin, our half brother, who is eight years younger than I am, also learnt to sail in Seaview and now has a flat here. He recently sailed from Auckland to Fiji on my eldest son's yacht.

Bram was drawn to the sea throughout his life, with vacations spent sea side in Ireland, Scotland and England. He was a strong swimmer, and he too enjoyed boating.

Fortunately, Bram was also a prolific and methodical note taker, thorough and meticulous in everything he did. For Bram's father, Abraham Sr, and Bram himself, note taking and record keeping was de rigueur at Dublin Castle, and for Bram as clerk of court.

Surviving ledgers from the Lyceum Theatre illustrate Bram's obsessive organisational skills. Throughout eight trans-Atlantic tours to America with the Lyceum, besides handling the press for Henry Irving and Ellen Terry, Bram kept tidy records of travel schedules, hundreds of people on the payroll, train cars full of costumes and stage sets, hotel reservations, and countless other decisions to be made every day, all the while meticulously tracking expenses in order to turn a profit. The ability to balance the books (no pun intended) carried through to his son Noel Stoker, as well as his great-grandsons in their careers as chartered accountants.

I first spoke to Noel (Dobbs) about publishing the Journal a couple of years ago. I had heard and read references to Bram's 'journal' and to his diary, and my mind raced with the possibilities: were the notes of a personal nature? What secrets about Bram would they reveal? How could I do the subject justice?

Literary dissection and research of this Journal, exploring this 'virgin territory', has given me a deeper understanding of Bram than I thought might be possible. Prior to immersing myself in this project, I relied on information gathered from others: family stories, biographies and Bram's published work. Over the years, I recognised that certain inaccuracies had been circulated as facts. There are contradictory dates in some of the Stoker biographies, and a few family stories told in North America don't line up with the British versions.

Theories have been tossed around about the nature of the man, Bram Stoker; these I have always taken with a grain of salt, and the majority have been discounted. The opportunity to read Bram's notes first-hand, and draw my own conclusions, has been an unparalleled experience, enhanced by working with Elizabeth Miller and with Bram's great-grandsons, Noel and Robin.

There was no question that I would need help to properly decipher and interpret the material, and my friend Elizabeth was the obvious choice, both for me and for Noel, given her recent involvement in the publication of Bram's notes for *Dracula*. Considering the earlier impact of the 'discovery' of those 124 pages of notes, I wondered whether this Journal could have equal significance. There were important issues to be resolved. Posthumous copyright laws are complicated. Which country's laws could protect the notes from public domain? What type of publisher would appreciate this work, and be able to best guide us towards presenting it most suitably for public consumption?

I waited anxiously for Noel to have the pages carefully photographed. I will never forget the day the images of the Journal pages arrived in my computer's inbox. I really had no idea about the contents. Would there be enough material to be of interest to the literary world? I couldn't wait to see it for myself.

Glancing through the images, I felt a measure of relief, as I realised I could actually read much of the handwriting. I settled in to read a few of the entries very closely. At that point I was struck by a sobering thought: these were the pure, unfiltered and private thoughts of my great-grand-uncle, entrusted to me 140 years later. It would be up to me to prepare and present the material to the world, a huge responsibility considering the author. Although known universally as *Dracula*'s creator, Bram Stoker himself has remained a stranger to most of the people who have read and enjoyed *Dracula*. I knew that was about to change.

After my wife Jenne and I pored over the pages on the computer monitor, we were eager to call Elizabeth and describe what we had, and send her the file. Needless to say she was very excited, but her excitement turned to frustration as her computer was unable to download the large file. So, I burned the file onto a disk and rushed it off to Toronto via second-day air.

While I waited for Elizabeth to receive the disk, I did my best to read the different entries. Some seemed hopeless. Because these notes were made for his use only, Bram took no great care with his penmanship. According to his 'time stamp', memos were written late at night, by candle or lamplight – and on some pages Bram's handwriting is little better than chicken scratch. As I read lines over and over again, I began to get a clearer understanding of the words, but the idioms, the stories in dialect, the nineteenth-century slang were all daunting. Why did Bram record so many seemingly random occurrences? And who were the people he mentioned?

Bram's system of recording his notes suited his purpose, and he gave no consideration to our plight. He used little punctuation, and unless he was quoting someone else, or transcribing from another source, i.e. his diary or 'pocketbook', the notes were often cryptic. Initially, it was somewhat disappointing that many entries merely recorded sights and sounds, but that was shortsighted. Gradually, it dawned on me; I was really getting to know Bram in the context of his world in Dublin. I began to appreciate the significance of the Journal, not only in what it reveals about the author, but as a time capsule of sorts, a slice of life in Dublin in the 1870s, seen through his eyes. And just as important was the realisation that a great deal of Bram's fiction was drawn from his own experiences and surroundings. The parallels were obvious.

What was it about these particular incidents that made him want to remember them? I began to visu-alise situations, as I imagined he would have observed them: interactions on the street, at work in the

Petty Sessions court proceedings, or, for that matter, anywhere during his normal daily routine. It is impossible to know whether his notes were embellished, or if he was recording accurately. His ability seamlessly to blend reality with fiction was one of his strongest skills as a writer, perfected in *Dracula*. This notebook seems to have been his training ground.

As Elizabeth, Jenne and I worked, it became evident that, for us, each entry represented a mystery waiting to be solved, often an abbreviation of a much more complicated scenario. Deciphering each entry required the mindset of treasure hunters and archaeologists, as we searched for connections to lead us to 'the rest of the story'. In many cases, two or three sentences and a date led to numerous newspaper articles, and we happened upon fascinating bits of history we would never otherwise have encountered.

Elizabeth's prior experience transcribing Bram's notes for *Dracula* and her familiarity with his handwriting were invaluable. Even so, there are some words we just could not decipher with confidence. In the beginning, every <xxx> haunted me, but eventually I got comfortable with the notion that we would just have to leave some puzzles for the next generation of researchers. Surely Bram never dreamt anyone would spend so much time analysing and theorising about any of his work, much less this collection of raw data. However, for our purposes, the fact that his thoughts were captured unfiltered and unedited made the notes more alluring.

I was eager to formulate an amateur character profile of Bram from his notes: not only the who, what, when and where of growing up as Bram Stoker in Dublin, but also to understand his humour, inspirations and personal values. I have long known he was much more than just the man who introduced *Dracula* to the world of Gothic literature and the horror genre. Bram provided us with some very interesting stories about his early childhood, but between age 7 and when he moved to London in 1878, very little has been known, other than where he lived, worked and went to school. He revealed some of himself in his *Personal Reminiscences of Henry Irving*, but that covered the London years. As I would soon see, the missing Dublin years were laid out here, recorded in his own hand.

Over the past few years I became much better acquainted with another one of Bram's great-grand-sons, Robin MacCaw. I learned that Robin shares a similar interest with me, to learn as much as possible about Bram from his writings. As it turns out Robin is quite fond of a particular poem from the Journal. He had photocopied the poem 'Pain & Bravery' (2), and his daughter Mimi had it framed so it can sit on his desk. I asked Robin to share with me his particular connection to Bram through the poem:

> I am able to connect with Bram through his poem 'Pain & Bravery', written a week before his twenty-fifth birthday, which I feel encapsulates his life. The piece may or may not have been autobiographical, but I see in it a reflection of his own strong character. Bram knew great pain and frustration as a sickly bed-bound child for seven years; and would demonstrate his own bravery in later life – for example when he dived into the Thames River in 1882 in an attempt to rescue a drowning soldier.

We know that Bram had at least one diary, possibly even more. He may also have had more than one commonplace notebook to work from. Knowing now how these notes were woven into his fiction, it makes sense that Bram would have continued recording his thoughts beyond the last date in this book. Have any other notes survived? Bram and Florence moved several times after relocating to London in 1878, and there is no telling what may have been lost in the fire at the Lyceum Theatre. Nonetheless, it is also quite possible that another notebook or diary will turn up, just as the notes for *Dracula* surfaced. Papers could be sitting in a box, or on a shelf, unnoticed, or are perhaps a collector's prize possession. Whatever the case, I encourage anyone who may know of their whereabouts to make them known. I am extremely interested in learning as much as I can about this complex and interesting man, and welcome the assistance and participation of people who share my focus. Elizabeth and I do not have a monopoly on Bram Stoker research, just a healthy appetite for more.

For now, we have done as much as we can. We have come to the end, but we are far from finished. We trust the transcription and our analysis will stimulate others to continue our work. Meanwhile additional information on the Journal, the Stoker family and *Dracula* will be posted on the Bram Stoker Estate website (www. bramstokerestate.com).

As fate would have it, not only did these notes survive, but thanks to Noel Dobbs's generosity, they will live on and flourish. No longer sequestered in a private collection, they have been given a new life; I am honoured to have been part of the process.

*Dacre Stoker*
January 2012

# ⊷ INDEX ⊷